ABOUT THE AUTHOR

Lowell Dunston served forty-nine years as an Adventist pastor, teacher, and administrator in the Mid-America Union, Lake Union, Pacific Union, and North Pacific Union Conferences. He received his education in Adventist schools, graduating with a bachelor's degree at Pacific Union College, and a master of divinity degree from Andrews University. His passion for education led him to attend eight summer sessions at Walla Walla University, focusing on courses in reading and writing. His last assignment was at Cypress Adventist School, for which he wrote a school history. He and his wife Carroll live in Everett, Washington.

Faith Trek
Into the
Unknown

LOWELL DUNSTON

TEACH Services, Inc.
PUBLISHING
www.TEACHServices.com • (800) 367-1844

World rights reserved. This book or any portion thereof may not be copied or reproduced in any form or manner whatever, except as provided by law, without the written permission of the publisher, except by a reviewer who may quote brief passages in a review.

The author assumes full responsibility for the accuracy of all facts and quotations as cited in this book. The opinions expressed in this book are the author's personal views and interpretations, and do not necessarily reflect those of the publisher.

This book is provided with the understanding that the publisher is not engaged in giving spiritual, legal, medical, or other professional advice. If authoritative advice is needed, the reader should seek the counsel of a competent professional.

Copyright © 2024 Lowell Dunston

Copyright © 2024 TEACH Services, Inc.

ISBN-13: 978-1-4796-1780-7 (Paperback)

ISBN-13: 978-1-4796-1781-4 (ePub)

Library of Congress Control Number: 2024919339

All scripture quotations, unless otherwise indicated, are taken from the King James Version.

Scripture quotations marked ESV are taken from The Holy Bible, English Standard Version. ESV® Text Edition: 2016. Copyright © 2001 by Crossway Bibles, a publishing ministry of Good News Publishers.

Scripture quotations marked NIV are taken from the Holy Bible, New International Version®, NIV® Copyright ©1973, 1978, 1984, 2011 by Biblica, Inc.® Used by permission. All rights reserved worldwide.

Scripture quotations marked Phillips are taken from The New Testament in Modern English, copyright 1958, 1959, 1960 J.B. Phillips and 1947, 1952, 1955, 1957 The Macmillian Company, New York. Used by permission. All rights reserved.

DEDICATION

Faith Trek Into the Unknown is dedicated to a host of people who helped me in the process of composing this book.

First is my wife, Carroll Dunston, whose considerable writing skill and encouragement launched me on my way. Unfortunately, as 2023 dawned and I was recovered enough to begin the writing process again, Carroll's Macular Degeneration had increased to where she was unable to see my computer screen.

Early in 2023, enter Rick Roberts, former teaching friend and computer tech, bringing a refurbished HP computer with large screen and Windows 10. Rick transferred my total book data to my new machine, and thanks to him, I was ready to resume writing—almost! My stroke had maimed my left hand, so I was faced with continuing my writing project with just one good hand—my right one!

Next, I include my two English-major sisters, Ellen Roe and Helen Sage, both tirelessly pushing me through the writing process. I attached my chapter drafts to each weekly family letter getting much valuable feedback. My sisters encouraged me to include earlier chapters of my faith walk through life to lay the foundation for the finale of my faith walk in the Cypress years. Helen faithfully called every noon to encourage me across the finish line! It was Helen who found a publisher in TEACH Services, Inc., for which I'll be forever grateful.

Writing on new equipment, mountains of tech problems stacked up leaving me very frustrated. It was at that point that Edson Carbajal, recent Walla Walla University engineering grad and computer tech extraordinaire, entered our lives. Working nearby at Boeing, he would drop by after work and in minutes solve what seemed like hours of challenges. I'm very indebted to Edson for getting a final draft in place and sent off to the publisher.

In addition, I want to thank many other family members and friends who read my drafts, liked my stories, and encouraged me to publish.

TABLE OF CONTENTS

1. Songs in the Night 13
2. My Life's Beginnings 19
3. Finding Joy in the Adventist Journey 22
4. My School Days Arrive 30
5. Growing Pains 34
6. 1957 – Faith Epic - 1 39
7. 1957 – Faith Epic - 2 42
8. Family Survival 44
9. Doors of Providence 46
10. My PUC Finale 48
11. Faith Trek into the Unknown 50
12. Andrews Challenges 53
13. Stepping into Pastoral Life — 1 57

14. Stepping into Pastoral Life — 2 60
15. Great Expectations 64
16. Becoming a Teacher Myself 70
17. On the Air in Muncie, Indiana. 72
18. Attack on Our Sons 74
19. Deodora Memories 78
20. Richland Outreach 83
21. Washington D.C., Here We Come! 86
22. God's School 90
23. Puget Sound Adventures 94
24. Cypress Money Challenges and Miracles 97
25. Jack and Jill Must Have Play 102
26. Keep Those School Vans Going 105
27. The Cypress Paint Party. 109
28. "It's A Small World" 113
29. "When They Ring Those Golden Bells" 116
30. Catching the Beat of Adventist Education 119
31. Can I Come to Your School? 122
32. The Adventist Dilemma. 126
33. Epilogue: A Millennium of Affirmation. 131

PREFACE

This book was born as a part of the 75th anniversary project of the Green Lake Church of Seventh-day Adventists. Having served as principal of Cypress Adventist School for nearly two decades, I was asked to do my best to reconstruct the history of Cypress Adventist School (CAS).

In the fall of 2022, I began this writing project on my trusty old HP computer with Windows 7. The progression of my neurological condition challenged me, but I was blessed by the skills of my English major wife, Carroll, who had considerable writing-editing-proof reading experience. I composed roughly half of my manuscript when a sudden stroke halted my work. For the next six weeks I was confined to hospital rehab having to relearn many basic skills. My story will continue in chapter one of my book.

1.
SONGS IN THE NIGHT

I will never forget October 14, 2022. That fall season I'd felt an urge, actually a compulsion, to begin writing a memoir of my life, much of it centered in the arena of Adventist Education. Sitting in my powerchair, working on my memoir at my computer, I dozed for a few minutes. On waking, I knew something was wrong! My head was aching! My left hand was numb, catching in the doorway as I tried to exit my study in my power chair. When I entered the family room, my brother-in-law said, "Lowell, your speech is slurred!"

Had I suffered a stroke? My wife soon came home from grocery shopping. There was a quick consensus that I had indeed had a stroke! Next thing I knew was the 911 call. Hands placed me on a stretcher, loading me into the aid car! It was comforting when the EMTs allowed

> *Then in the long, lonely night hours, songs of my childhood suddenly began popping into my head!*

my wife to enter and sit beside me. It was a rough ride to the hospital. First, to the ER, then an MRI, then a CT scan. "You've indeed had a stroke! You face a few days in the hospital, then on to rehab."

Suddenly my world was turned upside-down! What would become of me—of us? At that moment a Bible verse surfaced in my brain: "**My times are in your hands**" **(Ps. 31:15).** It was then that I realized that everything would be OK! My life was in God's hands!

Three helpless days in the hospital! Five long weeks in rehab! Rehab days were packed full: PT strength-building exercises, OT coordination training, speech therapy—eating, drinking, swallowing practice; but the nights were something else! At first, I couldn't even read—let alone sleep, just lie awake … hours on end! Then in the long, lonely night hours, songs of my childhood suddenly began popping into my head! What an inspiration! What a blessing! Several were duets that my brother and I had sung together.

Take up Your Cross

I walked one day along a country road,
And there a stranger journeyed too.
Bent low beneath the burden of His load,
It was a cross, a cross I knew.

Chorus:
Take up your cross and follow Me,
I hear the blessed Savior say,
How can I make a lesser sacrifice,
When Jesus gave His all?

My cross I'll carry till the crown appears,
The way I journey soon will end.
When God, Himself, will wipe away all tears,
And friend have fellowship with friend.

                      (Alfred Henry Ackley, 1922. Public domain.)

Speak, My Lord

"Hear the Lord of harvest sweetly calling,
'Who will come and work for Me today?
Who will come and bring the lost and dying?
Who will point them to the narrow way?'

Chorus:
Speak, My Lord, Speak to me.
Speak, and I'll be quick to answer Thee.
Speak, My Lord. Speak, My Lord.
Speak, and I will answer, 'Lord, send me.' "

                              (George Bennard, public domain.)

Then came a song that Mrs. Gearhardt, my primary grade teacher, loved to sing.

Living for Jesus

Living for Jesus, a life that is true,
Striving to please Him in all that I do;
Yielding allegiance, glad hearted and free,
This is the pathway of blessing for me.

Chorus:
O Jesus, Lord and Savior, I give myself to Thee,
For Thou, in Thy atonement, didst give Thyself for me;
I own no other Master, my heart shall be Thy throne;
My life I give, henceforth to live, O Christ, for Thee alone.

(Thomas O. Chisholm, 1917. Public domain.)

Our Gilbert Creek Church was part of a multi-church district. Jess and Ruth Gearhart led us in favorite songs until the pastor arrived. Some songs I remember very well:

"When the Roll is Called Up Yonder"
"In the Garden"
"Shall We Gather at the River"
"In a Little While We're Going Home"
"Over Yonder"

Such singing over time thoroughly embedded Adventist beliefs deeply into our souls!

Then there's the influence of Gladstone Camp Meeting and the songs of the Junior Pavilion:

"Christ for Me"
"The Captain Calls for You"
"Every Day with Jesus"

Songs from academy chapel had their influence, too. One that especially touched my heart and strengthened my commitment was:

"I'll Be True, Precious Jesus"

Songs in the night from childhood years became a powerful source of comfort. They sweetened the long, lonely, difficult hours of my recuperation as nothing else could.

In addition to songs from my childhood, stories of God's special leading throughout my life surfaced clearly in my mind. Since my left hand remained partly paralyzed, the rest of my memoir poured out through only my right hand!

Is it really a surprise that my brother, my two sisters, and I all followed my mother into the teaching field of service, working mainly in the Adventist system of education? Day by day, and year by year, our lives were programmed and powerfully influenced by the messages of song. Our mother died prematurely at the age of seventy. On the resurrection morning, she will be both gratified and proud that her four children combined to give a century of service, mostly to Adventist Education.

2.
MY LIFE'S BEGINNINGS

Tales of my early days come from my Dunston uncles and my Grandmother Dunston, who lived with us for some months around the birth of my little sister, Helen. My grandmother remembered that I was so fascinated with a baby sister that I wanted a closer look. I climbed up on the bassinet, pulling the baby, the bassinet and all over on the floor!

When asked what I would like to be when I grew up, I answered, "A singer and a fighter." Those words were partly prophetic. Soon afterwards, when having a disagreement with my older brother, Loren, I chose physical force to settle our problem. It must have been near Christmas time because, to mask my brother's crying, I burst into singing, "All is calm, all is bright," in my loudest little boy soprano voice.

My brother's beautiful alto harmonized wonderfully with my boy soprano. I'll never forget our first public performance. For an MV (Missionary Volunteers) program, our family was to demonstrate a family worship scene. My parents, who were quite the organizers, had everything choreographed perfectly. The only problem was that, when I saw about 75 people in the audience, our duet became a tearful version of "Always Cheerful."

Our singing continued at home, Sabbath School, and church. My favorite music memory was singing a duet version of "Luther's Cradle Hymn," complete with chorus, for a school Christmas program choreographed by my mother.

My parents sacrificed to keep the four of us in church school. Our cars were used cars, our furniture and carpets were worn. However, most of our school years I remember as a delightful, happy experience! We had warm, caring teachers who reinforced the sense of the Adventist message and mission that we caught from our parents at home.

Of first importance to our family was the opportunity for Adventist Education. We uprooted and moved three times for that reason: first to Gilbert Creek, Oregon, for nine grades, next to Laurelwood for academy, then to Pacific Union College for higher education options. Those were challenging times for our parents: selling houses, moving, and sometimes my dad temporarily separated from family—all aimed in the best interest of us children and our future.

We grew up hearing stories of our parents' own desire to gain a Christian education that had been dashed by the Great Depression. For us, there was never a question about whether we would go to college.

That option was embedded early in our psyches—go to college and prepare to serve the Lord!

The chapters that follow flow out of my life experiences: growing-up years of preparation, seventeen years working as a pastor, and thirty-two years serving as a teacher and school principal. They are penned with the hope that you too are discovering JOY in your Adventist journey and that you are finding that "All his biddings are enablings" (Ellen White, *Christ's Object Lessons*, p. 333).

3.
FINDING JOY IN THE ADVENTIST JOURNEY

FIRST MEMORIES

My first sense of Adventist community came in my fourth year when we moved from Southern California to Rose Lodge, Oregon (a few miles inland from what is now Lincoln City). That sense of community was centered in Sabbath.

ROSE LODGE

1. Sabbath Prep: Mom made cinnamon rolls for Sabbath breakfast and crescent rolls for lunch. We had homemade gluten or baked beans, potato salad and cake, cookies or pie. My brother and I mopped floors, my sisters did the weekly dusting. My little sister and I had the big job of shoe polishing (black, brown, white, and blue).

2. Our small church Sabbath School was special: singing and acting out "Head, Shoulders, Knees and Toes" faster and faster until some of the littler ones fell down. Sand boxes with all the cut outs illustrated the lesson.

3. Church: we always sat near the front as my dad was an elder and my mom often played the piano. Mom was creative: she carried small rainbow tablets from which she created origami magic. Her gold Schaeffer Eversharp with red-colored lead went up and down the row (each kid having five minutes). Our pew always increased in size as other children joined our family row, which was more exciting than most.

4. Sabbath afternoons: There were seven to eight families with kids of various ages. The moms pooled their Sabbath food, and we all headed for Road's End beach for a delightful afternoon. We didn't mind having sand in our potato salad as we were with friends. After lunch, there was a long walk, looking for agates and whole sand dollars. Sabbath protocol allowed pants to be rolled up to our knees for limited wading. When one over-eager kid got wet to his arm pits, the consequence was to sit with the "old folks" with a blanket wrapping his body for the rest of the day.

GILBERT CREEK – WILLAMINA, OREGON

In 1947, we moved to a rural Adventist logging community with about a hundred Seventh-day Adventists. There I started school in a two-room log schoolhouse (about thirty kids grades 1–10).

There was a strong sense of community there. In the big snow year of 1948, the whole valley was snowed in. Off-work dads descended on the school for days, cut a great amount of firewood to keep the two rooms warm, made a toboggan and a bobsled, and did extended recess with us kids.

> *The moms pooled their Sabbath food, and we headed for the beach. We didn't mind having sand in our potato salad as we were with friends.*

I came from a singing family. I was a boy-soprano; my brother had a wonderful harmonizing alto. Our older sister, Ellen, was a special asset. She could transpose and play the piano in any key. My duet debut with my brother dissolved in stage fright at the sight of the audience. However, we kept on singing, performing often in our little church.

Sabbath afternoons the youth of the community often walked up our hill to climb the trail up Mt. Darling, which rose behind our house. The Seventh-day Adventist sawmill sat at the top of the mountain.

LAURELWOOD

When my older sister was ready for 10th grade, we moved to Laurelwood. Most of the Seventh-day Adventist kids walked to school together. It was at Laurelwood that I first caught a sense of Adventist mission. For two winters of MV meetings, village folk filled the academy chapel balcony to hear the continued stories by Don Lee and Genevieve Kime, missionaries to the Far East, telling their stories of God's miraculous care and deliverance during the Japanese and then Communist occupations of Asia.

ANGWIN, CALIFORNIA, PACIFIC UNION COLLEGE

Before my 8th grade year, my family moved to Angwin, California, for Christian education options for all four of us kids, enabling all of us to stay at home. Once again, Sabbath became central to my sense of Adventist community. The Healdsburg bell tolled the arrival of Sabbath hours for all of Howell Mountain. Friday evening vespers in Irwin Hall Chapel brought the Seventh-day Adventist family close together. KPUC AM radio (later KANG FM) broadcast vesper services to the area. Those were powerful moments:

"Again, as evening's shadow falls,
We gather in these hallowed walls;
And vesper hymn and vesper prayer
Rise mingling on the holy air."

(Samuel Longfellow. 1859. Public Domain.)

Then C. Warren Becker or Lois Mae Stauffer charmed us with an organ rendition on "old windy," the cherished pipe organ. Often a college teacher shared a lesson from their life experience. Those became special times for building a sense of both Adventist community and Adventist mission.

Another major event was Alumni Home Coming weekend each April. The high point was the lighting of the missionary map. While

Helen Matheson read the name of every PUC alumnus serving overseas, Jack Craver lit a light for them on the world map. Seeing that event for ten years instilled a desire in me to experience Adventist world mission—a dream that took forty-five years to fulfill.

OAMC

I joined the OAMC (Oregon Adventist Men's Chorus) in 2002. When plans were announced for "Mission to Romania" coming in April 2009, and again in 2014, I was eager to sign up. Words fail to convey the amazing experience of singing to packed houses in most of the major opera houses and cathedrals of Romania, bringing a whole new conception of Adventism to that country. The Romanian music ministry now stands on its own with yearly "Men's Chorus" festivals touching a country hungry for the gospel.

General Conference in the Georgia Dome beckoned the OAMC next. Worshiping on Sabbath with 70,000 Adventists from around the world was an amazing experience! The OAMC sang three times in the GC venue. At our final concert, a delegate from Africa approached us saying, "You must come to Africa, join with our men's chorus groups and take this mission to our country." That's how the "International Brotherhood Tour" was born!

"Mission to Africa" took place in 2012. At our first lunch, I sat by the oldest African member of the Botswana Chorus. I'll never forget his words. "You'll never know what you Americans coming means to us Africans. This is the first time we 'blacks' have ever been on an equal footing with whites." Instantly, I knew why I went to Africa. We rode on the same busses, ate together, shared rooms together, stood shoulder to shoulder on most of the major opera house stages of South Africa. Near the end of our trip, Bro. D, my bus mate across the aisle, said, "For years we Africans have longed to join in ministry with our white Seventh-day Adventist brothers. You Americans coming has made that happen. You have helped us to declare to our whole country that Adventists are not racist." Brother D died last summer. I'm so glad that we could help him and others of our African brothers experience equality and oneness in Christ that they had desired for so long!

MISSION TO UKRAINE – 2017

In the fall of 2016, the OAMC got the call, "Come to Ukraine and help us!" Our first challenge was to learn five songs in Ukrainian, a language which belongs to the Slavic family and uses the Cyrillic alphabet. We arrived in Kyiv in June 2017. Many of the locals were students from the Adventist university where we stayed. The national orchestra had been laid off for the summer, so about forty of them (many who were non-Christian atheists) made up the core of our orchestra. We booked concerts in six cities. Most memorable was Mariupol, just a few miles from the Russian occupied zone. The Seventh-day Adventist church there had only thirty-five members and very limited resources. They were fearful that the concert in this city of a half million would be a "no show" embarrassment. Lev, our Ukrainian director, felt that God had specifically led him to book a concert there.

When we arrived at the city center square, a huge military parade was just ending. They were celebrating the third anniversary of driving out the Russian invasion. A huge bandstand had been erected across the main entrance. A loud pop music concert was in progress. Our fifty-piece orchestra, 100 singers, plus the set-up crew got more attention than we knew. An hour later, the opera hall seating 850 people was jam packed. People were sitting on tiered steps, standing wherever they could. We learned later that 250 people were turned away. Mariupol was the most powerful concert of all. When Lev directed the final number, "Prayer for the Ukraine," people stood with tears flowing and waving Ukrainian flags. Lev told us afterwards that the mayor had tried to stop our concert by blocking the main entrance, but God overruled. He said, "If you ever wished to witness a miracle like first century Pentecost, you just saw one tonight!" The Seventh-day Adventist opera tenor who traveled with us wrote: "Your coming to join forces with us, singing in the largest halls of the major cities of our country has forever changed how Ukrainians view Adventists."

CONCLUSION

From what I've written here, some of you may think that I view our church only through "rose-colored glasses." I've been a Seventh-day Adventist worker for almost fifty years. I've earned my share of "battle scars." During one of those trying times, I got some priceless advice: "Lowell, every institution on earth is a human one. Humans make mistakes. You've got to look beyond the trauma of the moment for the bigger mission that God has in store for each of us."

It is true. Humans do make mistakes, but we all have choices. We can choose to wallow in our pain and become bitter or we can choose to go forward, eager to see what doors God might open for us in the future! I'm glad I took that advice from a friend. Today, I am concerned that many Adventists spend too much time viewing the "troubles of the church" via social media, thereby missing out in the "joy found in the journey" in being meaningfully involved in Adventist mission. I conclude with a verse from Heb. 12:14, Phillips translation.

"Be careful that none of you fails to respond to the grace which God gives, for if he does there can very easily spring up in him a bitter spirit which is not only bad in itself but can also poison the lives of many others."

My prayer for each of us today is that we will choose to find the *joy* awaiting us in the Adventist journey here below, finding it to be a *foretaste of eternal joys to come!*

4.
MY SCHOOL DAYS ARRIVE

I grew up in a family committed to chasing the best possible Adventist Education options for their children. My mother, having had two years of "normal training" (the designation refers to schools established primarily to train elementary-level teachers) and teaching a one room, eight-grade school, was an ideal person to guide my educational beginnings in first grade. For second grade, I joined my older sister and brother in a two-room log schoolhouse in northwest Oregon. My parents purchased forty acres of timberland just above the Gilbert Creek School property.

I loved my teacher, Mrs. Gerhardt. She enjoyed singing. Even though seventy-five years have passed, I still remember the songs that she taught us: "Hold the Fort, for I Am Coming," "Living for Jesus," and "I Would Be True." Our school was in the country, so God's second book of nature was central in our curriculum. Though having few educational resources, we learned to be resourceful. Front and back walls contained black chalkboards, where we often did math drills. The north wall was all windows. When we needed things to do, we looked in the teacher's file box, found something to copy, paperclipped the master to a white piece of paper, went to a window, and traced a copy for ourselves.

About fifteen students were in grades one through five, so we had enough students to have two sides for most recess games. The school was heated by wood stoves. In wintertime, a sheet metal shield around the stove served as a protective barrier. Winter recesses were a wonderful break! OSHA hadn't banned snowballs yet! Snowball fights, sledding, and tobogganing made for a rosy-cheeked group of scholars! On return to class, we hung hats, gloves, outer pants, and coats over the shield to dry and provide steam to humidify the classroom.

The old log schoolhouse had no running water! Hence, we took turns at recess taking pails to walk and see the neighbor for water. She loved children and treated us to lemon drops. With no running water at school, there were no bathrooms—only cold outhouses! Rolls of toilet paper were kept inside shortening cans. For a backup supply in an emergency, there were Sears and Montgomery Wards catalogs.

All students had jobs to end the day. Older students filled the wood box for the next day. Some students swept floors; some wiped blackboards clean; some pounded chalk erasers on the outside walls of both school and woodshed, giving walls a fresh whitewash each and every day!

After my third grade, the Adventist sawmill, which was the mainstay of the community, moved to Bandon, Oregon, for a larger timber supply. Much of the school family would move with the sawmill. Would the school close? After a careful count and with a new family with four kids moving in, there were still seventeen potential students. The challenge of finding a teacher was solved when Grandma Miller agreed to come out of retirement for a year. My mother would assist her in the afternoons.

Mrs. Miller demanded strict order. To enter the class, we had to line up by grade, get in step with the old seventy-eight phonograph marching record, and enter the classroom in an orderly manner.

The most memorable program of my elementary years happened that Christmas. My mother choreographed the program. Every student had a personal part, a recitation, a vocal solo or duet, and group carols. My brother and I sang a rare arrangement of "Luther's Cradle Hymn," complete with chorus. That song has stayed with me for all these succeeding years!

Recently I reread Jesse Stuart's *The Thread that Runs So True*. In this story of teaching in a small school in West Virginia and how it excelled over larger schools, we find an example of what happens in many a small Adventist school. The quality in an educational program is often found in the strong relationships of cooperation and comradeship that develop between teacher and students in these intimate situations. That explains the dynamic of success found in many small Adventist schools.

Though my educational beginnings were in small, humble places, I didn't grow up feeling deprived. I had a good foundation. Teachers, students, and parents were all united in the process, and God was very present as He guided in all the details. Together we learned that "All His biddings are enablings" (*Christ's Object Lessons*, p. 333).

5.
GROWING PAINS

"I don't want to move! I'm happy here at Laurelwood Elementary. I have lots of friends. I like my teachers. We have summer and fall jobs, too. I don't want to uproot again and move to California." My little sister, Helen, also felt quite comfortable with her circle of friends and didn't relish uprooting and starting over again.

It was early summer in 1954. My older sister, Ellen, had just graduated from Laurelwood Academy with honors and was college bound. She was not excited about going to Walla Walla at the time but was more interested in going to Pacific Union College located at Angwin, California.

In addition, Oregon Conference was bringing in a new administration to Laurelwood Academy and threatening to close the school to village students, forcing all academy students to live in the dorm. Imagine how the village families (one third of the students) felt after moving to the area to have access to a K-12 Christian education program!

My parents were firmly rooted in the opposition. My father searched Ellen White's writings and had his quotations ready. I'll always remember the lengthy and tense evening meeting in the old Laurelwood Church. As a future eighth grader, this would be my first experience observing denominational politics in action! It would generate feelings and implications for attitudes that would affect the rest of my life!

I could feel the tension in that packed room! Many village people were angry. Some of the speeches were *hot!* My dad waited for the anger to be vented. After some time, he rose to speak. He spoke calmly, yet with confidence. He summarized the reasons for families moving to the area for an affordable Christian education for the whole family. He talked about the sacrifices many had made to move there. He read some Ellen G. White statements supporting the concept of family involvement in the education of children and of the dangers of congregating large groups of youth together without parental involvement. We were proud of his speech. However, some in the church were disappointed that he did not come to this crucial meeting ready to spearhead a rebellion.

It was obvious from the conference brethren's responses that the "die was cast" and that they were dead set on moving ahead with their plans to shut down the village option. From that night on, our family plans shifted and were centered on selling our place and moving to California.

We arrived in the intense heat of August. Homes to rent were very scarce. We put money down to rent a small house at the top of the hill on White Cottage Road. Then a visitor, Dr. Paul Quimby, came from the big house just down the street. He would become an important guardian of our family's welfare for many a year. He arranged for us to rent a large furnished unadvertised house just across the street. There were thirteen acres of apple orchard, grapes, and space for a garden. It suited us well.

Though this move provided quality Christian educational opportunities for all four of us kids, while we had money to enroll all of us in school, the move also brought many challenges and hurdles for our family to surmount. First, for this experiment to work, Dad (at least for the first year) had to return to his high paying job as millwright at the Oregon Alder and Maple Company in Oregon. He would have to batch for himself, and we would see him only a week at a time during vacations. We would have no car and would have to walk everywhere. Mom would have to care for all of us without a helpmate present. Fortunately, many others also had to walk, but many days the generous people of Howell Mountain offered rides to kids. The local Hilltop Grocery delivered groceries to homes. Every Sabbath the Quimbys dedicated the back seat of their Buick to my mom and my sisters for rides to church. My brother and I had to walk. Rainy Sabbaths we stayed home and listened to services on the radio. KPUC (KANG) radio became a familiar friend.

Though the move to a big class in a new school was a tough adjustment for me as an eighth grader, the Angwin setting began to make major influences in my life. Of first import was Friday night. The ringing of the Healdsburg bell ushered the Sabbath in to all of Howell Mountain. Friday evening vespers on KANG radio became a regular, sacred part of our lives. The artistry of C. Warren Becker playing "Again as Evening Shadow Falls" on "Old Windy," the pipe organ, each week ushered us into the very presence of God. Students and faculty offering Christian classics in instrument and voice created a love of great music. Faculty members sharing personal vesper messages created a powerful bond between student and teacher. As hard as basic survival was in our situation, slowly but surely, the powerful influences of the Howell Mountain community were making a lasting influence in our lives.

Entering ninth grade the next year was another challenging adjustment for me. I was still the new kid on the block, shy and non-athletic. At Prep there were several bullies to contend with—not a positive magnet to draw one to school. Due to family financial demands, Dad worked again in the Oregon mill away from home. Survival was tough! However, difficult as the year was, it ended with a silver lining. Elder Eugene Erickson was the speaker for spring week of prayer. He connected well with teens. Bible teacher Elder J. C. Miklos invited his students to a baptismal class. Both my brother and I responded. We were baptized together in the outdoor baptistery at PUC.

At the week of prayer's conclusion, it was announced that Elder Miklos would assume the principal position at Prep and Elder Erickson would become our new Bible teacher.

> *The room was a disaster! The floor was littered with paper-wads and spitballs!*

Fast forward a number of years. I was a senior theology-education major facing my first unit of micro-teaching! On a Friday afternoon, I met Elder Erickson in my old Bible classroom. The room was a disaster! The floor was littered with paper-wads and spitballs! "I'm sorry, Lowell, that you had to see this. The man ahead of you could not relate to teens. I'm required to leave you alone for the final period. When I told the kids that you were coming next week and that you had graduated from Prep, they thought that was cool. You are an authentic person. I don't expect any trouble. You'll do fine."

The next week did indeed go well. It *was* fine! And I treasured Elder Erickson's vote of confidence. Once again, I discovered that "All His biddings are enablings" (*Christ's Object Lessons*, p. 333).

6.
1957 - FAITH-EPIC-1

The year 1957 became an epic year in my personal faith journey! The summer began with the youth of Howell Mountain scrambling for jobs. I landed one working at the local Dude Ranch cleaning up around cabins before summer guests arrived. Sam Gramlich, brother-in-law of one of my best friends, was my boss. As July rolled around, the clean up work was done. Sam moved to the back property to operate heavy equipment to begin building another earthen dam for the community water supply. The owner took me by jeep to the dam site, commenting on the way that he liked my work and would keep me busy the rest of the summer.

The site for the new lake was cleared, and Sam drove the earthmover, spreading dirt for the new dam. My task was to lay rock across the inside face of the earthen fill. About noon, a white pickup arrived. The owner drove his jeep quickly to where I worked and said, "Hop in." We drove up to a shade tree where he explained that the state inspector had arrived. "When you see that rig arrive, you need to make yourself scarce. You're only sixteen; you're supposed to be eighteen to be around equipment. We want to avoid trouble. Eat your lunch while I talk to the inspector. I'll come get you when he leaves."

A cacophony of thoughts whirled in my head as I ate lunch. What should I do? I desperately needed work, but I was faced with a dilemma involving both me and my boss.

When he came back, I said, "We need to talk." All my hunches were correct. When I asked about the legality of my continuing my work, wondering if I should continue, He exploded. "You're fired! Get in the jeep." It was a wild ride down the mountain. He hastily wrote me a check, then said, "I thought you were my boy. If you keep letting this over-conscientiousness rule what you do, you'll be a nobody and never go anywhere in life."

I got on my bike and, in a daze, rode home, entered my room in the basement, dropped to my knees teary-eyed and said, "Lord, I don't want to be a nobody, but I had to do what I just did." After I calmed down, I went upstairs and told my mom what had happened. She agreed that I had done the right thing.

That evening, my friend, Delmer, dropped by. He said he had just quit a part-time summer job at the Angwin Book Bindery. He had been hired for a full-time job that would continue on through the winter. He advised me to arrive at 7:30 a.m. the next morning to apply for the bindery position. Arriving at the bindery bright and early, I was hired on the spot.

Since there were no textbooks that day to move from the basement to the check-in room (the main job I was hired for) my first assignment was to sweep the whole bindery by department sections. Everywhere were many trimmings from five paper cutters, strings from four sewing machines, and layers of dust. Oiled sweeping compound had to be spread on the wooden floor without getting any on book sections in various stages. My parents had fortunately instilled a good work ethic in the members of my family. After two days of my thorough sweeping, the four women supervisors declared that the bindery had never been so clean. They told the bindery manager, "You'd better keep that boy!" A temporary part-time job turned into a full-time summer job and continued into the school year as a permanent position where I filled in wherever needed.

In a few months, the miraculous workings of the Lord laid an epic foundation of trust that directed all my future life. A favorite Ellen White quotation became the motto of my life: "All His biddings are enablings" (*Christ's Object Lessons,* p. 333).

7.
1957- FAITH EPIC-2

My new bindery job helped the summer of 1957 to fly by. I loved my work there. Jack, a classmate and son of the manager, taught me many bindery jobs before he moved next door into an apprentice position in the machine shop. Even when my junior year of academy started, I was able to squeeze out about twenty hours a week for work.

With summer work and continued work into the fall, I built a significant work credit. All seemed to be going well. Then Christmas eve brought another crisis to our family. Late that afternoon, two men from college church furniture brought my dad home severely injured. In a freak accident, Dad had lost two fingers. The main breadwinner for our family was suddenly out of work and permanently disabled.

Post Christmas time was registration again at PUC Prep. I had more than enough credit to register, but what about my little sister with no parental income resources to help? Then the college business office sent me a terse letter, saying "You are being laid off from your bindery job immediately. We need your job for a college dorm student." I took the letter and handed it to Mr. Sherman, the very kind and mild-mannered bindery manager. He took a quick look, then red color inflaming his face, he said, "Who's the manager here anyway? Give me that letter!"

A few minutes later he returned from the business office all smiles. "You're not fired! You're one of my best workers. All you need to do is sign this paper that the credit you build up over what you need can be transferred to your little sister, Helen." Once again, I knew that Someone was looking out for both me and my family—Someone who could manage my challenges that seemed impossible to me and out of my control—Someone who was in charge of even the controlling hierarchy of the institution!

Again, I discovered that "All His biddings are enablings" (*Christ's Object Lessons*, p. 333).

Here's an interesting footnote: Three years later, my little sister, Helen, was hired in the sewing department—one of the most demanding of student jobs in the bindery. She quickly became the fastest and most accurate sewer in bindery history, and so much so that the sewing piecework rate had to be refigured because she was making too much money (at least the business office thought so)!

8.
FAMILY SURVIVAL

In the spring of 1957, my brother, Loren, graduated from PUC Prep ready to enter college. That summer he was hired at Hilltop Store, the village shopping place. The house next door was for rent, so we moved in. It was very convenient in many ways.

In Angwin tradition, the Hilltop Store opened for the convenience of Angwin shoppers at fifteen minutes after sundown every Saturday night. My brother was Saturday night cashier, and I was the bagboy. The parking lot was filled with cars by sundown. Knowing that we lived next door, horns began to honk as soon as sundown arrived. Our family traditions included sundown family worship with vesper hymns and a devotional thought. Honking horns did not bring a peaceful end to our Sabbath rest!

One warm Sabbath evening my brother had had enough! Striding into the parking lot, he yelled, "Our family happens to have sundown worship. You all know that Hilltop doesn't open until fifteen minutes after sundown. If you insist, we can start having sundown vespers right here in the parking lot!"

We then went inside to prepare for customers. Slowly and quietly the Howell Mountain Pharisees entered the store. The crowd was more subdued that night. The sound of sundown horns was heard no more! Their memory gradually faded into the woodwork.

> *One warm Sabbath evening my brother had had enough!*

One of the problems of my working in a college industry such as the well-paying Angwin Book Bindery (we had piece-work rates and made good wages) was the trouble of getting cash. Our family learned how to work the system and care for each other at the same time. I transferred tuition credit to my brother's account (also, to my little sister). He in turn gave me cash for clothes and personal items. That way I avoided alarming the business office that I had too much credit building up in my account and all of us siblings were able to stay in school.

While we learned to trust in God through difficult times ("All His biddings are enablings"), we also learned that God does indeed seem to bless those who learn to help themselves.

9.
DOORS OF PROVIDENCE

What should I do with my life? I was in my senior year at PUC Prep. Principal Miklos had given us a battery of tests: California Achievement and Aptitude tests and Kuder Occupation Interest Survey. In our small, intimate Spanish 2 class, we shared our profiles of results. Feedback and support from both teacher and trusted friends was much appreciated. My abilities and interests pointed me toward the teaching area, which was no surprise as I came from a teacher family: including my grandmother, mother, older sister, aunt, and uncle.

College registration was an exciting moment. I'd filled out my papers planning for a religion major, looking toward secondary teaching. Since I already had two years of Spanish, I'd put myself down for intermediate Spanish to finish my foreign language requirement in one more year.

When I entered the religion department to get an advisor check and signature, who should I meet but Dr. Quimby, a former neighbor and old family friend. Little did I know that this encounter would change the entire course of my life!

Dr. Quimby took a quick look at my papers and said, "We need to talk." He reminded me of my parents' sacrifice, of our family coming to PUC for us four kids to prepare for a place in the Lord's work. He strongly suggested that I change to a theology major, taking fifteen hours of Biblical Greek instead of nine hours of Spanish. "You'll have Dr. Maxwell for both Greek and Biblical Philosophy. He's the dean of religion and one of the best teachers in our PUC Bible Department. You'll never regret this change."

I'd never before considered preparing for being both a pastor and a teacher! This encounter was completely unexpected. I sensed that this advice could be providential and accepted it. I loved my two classes from Dr. Graham Maxwell, and he became one of the most significant mentors of my life.

In my academy years, I had begun reading Ellen White's writings for my private devotions. I remembered a classic statement, "As the will of man co-operates with the will of God, it becomes omnipotent. Whatever is to be done at His command may be accomplished in His strength. All His biddings are enablings" (*Christ's Object Lessons*, p. 333).

That quotation became a keynote for my life!

10.
MY PUC FINALE

It was the last week of my senior year at Pacific Union College. All the seniors had written comprehensive exams in their major fields. For the final step, I entered the theology department for orals in my major field. All the professors sat in a semi-circle facing me—not the most comfortable moment of my life!

After a brief introduction, the chair opened the floor for questions. Academic questions were minimal. I was asked for a few clarifications of details. Then the room went silent. Finally the chair cleared his throat and took the plunge. It went like this:

"Lowell, some of us are concerned about your future.... We don't see a young lady on your arm."

The air was suddenly sucked out of the room. No one spoke! Privately I was both stunned and angry at this sudden intrusion into my private life in front of the total faculty. If he was concerned about my social life, why hadn't he made an appointment and talked with me privately?

I will always treasure Professor Carl Coffman's magnanimous rescue. It went like this:

"Lowell and I have had private conversations about his future. He has done well in our program and has a strong sense of God's calling him into ministry, whether teaching or preaching. His future is not yet totally clear. At my advice, he has applied to the seminary, has been accepted, and is ready to pursue as God directs. As to the issue that was raised, there are as many young ladies on the Andrews campus as there are here. I don't think we need to worry about that issue."

Move four months into the future. One Friday early in the 1964 fall term at Andrews, my roommate and I shopped for groceries as our clothes dried in the laundromat next door. We met Marilyn, one of my PUC classmates, as we were shopping. She introduced us to her roommate, Carroll Blair. In time, she and I got acquainted and began dating. Our relationship progressed and, in the summer of 1965 on a moon-light night on the shore of Lake Michigan, Carroll agreed to become my wife.

The future steps of our lives are mostly unknown to us. Yet, as we follow God's leading, "All His biddings are enablings."

11.
FAITH TREK INTO THE UNKNOWN

It was Labor Day weekend in 1964. Spending all summer working off my PUC bill, I'd managed to save $150.00 in my checking account for the seminary entrance fee at Andrews University. I had pre-paid the $35.00 for the first month's rent for a room in the "bull pens" for single graduate guys and had my acceptance letter in hand. Friday morning, I loaded all my earthly possessions into my little Ford Falcon, left Angwin, California, and headed to Camino to spend my final weekend in California with my newlywed little sister, Helen, and my brother-in-law, Jerry, at his parent's place.

Bright and early Sunday, I headed east on Highway 50, beginning my journey eastward into the unknown. My financial plan for the trip was to charge my gas on my new Chevron credit card sent out to college grads. I had a promised job awaiting me in the Berrien Bindery. What more would I need? Little did I know!

Faintly at first, I heard a clicking and clacking sound in the engine as I climbed the summit of the Sierras. Coasting into Reno checking for a Sunday mechanic proved challenging. Most mechanics were off to the auto races. I finally found a backyard mechanic kid to tackle my problem. The rocker arms in my straight six were not getting sufficient oil and were beginning to wear. Since no mechanic and no parts were available, my choice was to move on east on I-80 and hope to reach Salt Lake City. I clicked and clacked my way across the hot desert reaching Salt Lake about midnight. Early Monday I found a mechanic who agreed to take an out-of-state check and fix my car for the $150.00 that I had.

Hoarding my small amount of cash for frugal meals, sleeping in my car at rest stops, I finally arrived at Andrews about midnight Thursday night. The campus being pitch black and looking uninhabited, I headed to Benton Harbor to find a tiny room taking $7.00 from the $10.00 that I had left. Not having had a shower for five days, I felt I should appear at Andrews the first time looking somewhat civilized.

Waking early Friday, I treated myself to breakfast with my last few dollars. It was with a heavy heart that I retraced the few miles back to Berrien Springs. I pulled into the seminary parking lot, said a silent prayer, took a few deep breaths, and walked into the seminary dean's office. I announced that I had just arrived to register for school. The dean found my papers, looked them over, and commented that my paperwork was in place. "Now I need $150.00 from you, then I'll sign the paper that will let you register for classes on Sunday."

My response stunned the dean. I told him that I didn't have any money, and out poured my tale of woe.

The dean responded, "I don't know what to do with people who just show up for school without any money. I'm sending you across the hall to the graduate dean. He seems to have a talent for working miracles for people with no money."

My apprehension grew as I waited, dreading going through all this again! I felt like heading back to California but remembered that doing so would be a denial of my whole last five-year faith journey! At that moment, I was warmly welcomed with a firm handshake by the graduate dean. Quickly looking over my papers, he commented, "You have good grades and great references. You're the kind of student we are looking for." Then smiling, he commented, "I understand you have a little money problem. That's something that I can help you with. I'm granting you $150.00 from the graduate scholarship fund. Here's the signed paper you need to register for classes on Sunday."

"All His biddings are enablings" (*Christ's Object Lessons*, p. 333).

These words penned by Ellen White so many years ago were not a myth. I had just discovered again that they indeed were *reality*. That's how my seminary saga began.

12.
ANDREWS CHALLENGES

I was about four weeks into my graduate school year at Andrews, and I loved my classes. My job in the Berrien Bindery was going well, I thought. One day the manager called me in. "Lowell, I'm going to have to lay you off. Work is drying up as we are entering a recession. I can only keep some full-time staff."

What was I going to do? At this time of year, all the good jobs on campus and in town were taken. Without a dependable car, my only option was to take a job on the night shift at College Wood Products—the place of least-liked jobs on campus. And of course, there was a pay cut. Even with two five-hour shifts during the week and nine hours on Sunday, I was running behind financially. Snow came early and trudging home in freezing weather near midnight plunged me into one of the darkest periods of my life. No human being knew about my situation as I did not feel comfortable talking about it.

Thanksgiving arrived. Fellow students talked excitedly about going home. I had nowhere to go and was out of both food and money. The factory shut down at 6:00 p.m. Thanksgiving eve. On an impulse, I went by the seminary mail boxes to check my cubby. Inside were some returned mid-term exams and a legal envelope with my name printed neatly. The envelope contained the following note: "Can a mother forget the baby at her breast and have no compassion on the child she has borne? Though she may forget, I will not forget you" (Isa. 49:15, NIV). It was an anonymous note, but inside was a crisp $10.00 bill. When I reached the stairs to my apartment, there sat a food box of essentials from a local Dorcas group. In my Friday's mail was a note from my older sister, Ellen, a new teacher struggling to make ends meet. The card read, "I was impressed that you needed money." Inside was a $35.00 check. I was in Michigan; she was in Oregon. Those three miracles let me know that I was not alone!

Michigan winter dragged on. My daily encouragement came from my stereo and sacred LP collection. Faith and courage both came by singing in Dr. Becker's Seminary Men's Chorus for Friday vespers, accompanied by the Pioneer Memorial Church organ. These things brought significant weekly staying power into my time of darkness.

Winter rolled on. With the coming of Christmas, students happily chatted about going home. Again, I had nowhere to go and faced working at CWP the whole vacation to be able to stay in school. Then there was pre-registration for second semester. The graduate dean called me in. "We've noticed your efforts to stay in school. I'm giving you another $150.00 scholarship to enable you to enroll for second semester." Thank you, Lord!

> "Lowell, you may wonder why it is so much easier for some than it is for you."

Christmas eve I trudged through the falling snow for about fifteen minutes to reach my apartment. I was feeling down and blue as home was 2000 miles away. As I stamped snow off on the side entry porch, Larry, my student landlord, called to me, "Lowell, my wife and I were just feeling sorry for ourselves that we could not do Christmas with either of our parents. Then we thought of you. We'd like you to be our Christmas dinner guest tomorrow."

Often, I wondered why I had to face all these difficulties and hardships. The answer came partly when I went to get second semester paperwork signed at the dean's office. Mrs. Jemison, the dean's secretary, called me in and offered this commentary:

"Lowell, some of us have noticed how hard you've worked to stay in school. You may wonder why it is so much easier for some than it is for you. The challenges that you're going through will make you a much more compassionate and understanding worker in God's cause."

One of my *life's callings* has been to raise scholarship funds for worthy students in three schools. I made a commitment to God to never turn away a parent or student who seriously desired a Christian education. Over the years God has blessed me in raising many thousands of dollars. I'm especially grateful to have been a catalyst in establishing a Hispanic scholarship fund in the NPUC (North Pacific Union Conference) to assist 100 students per year.

As I look back over the years, I can truly say both for myself and for many others, "All His biddings [*indeed*] are enablings" (*Christ's Object Lessons*, p. 333).

13.
STEPPING INTO PASTORAL LIFE-1

Carroll and I were newlyweds. I had just finished my last class, Field School of Evangelism, in Houston, Texas, and we were headed where I would have my first work assignment. Our pastoral internship was to be with Pastor and Mrs. W. Arden Clarke in Omaha, Nebraska.

Carroll landed an exciting job at the Pathology Center at Methodist Hospital. Omaha was a large city with a 500-member church, plus many Seventh-day Adventists would come from smaller towns in the surrounding areas for surgery. For my first day on the job, Pastor Clarke took me on a whirlwind trip around the city, checked in at all thirteen hospitals, found the clergy parking, checked the records office for Seventh-day Adventist patients, making a brief visit to each one—a lot to remember for one day! Two to three days each week, that would be my task.

When I remarked that I had never done hospital visiting, Pastor Clarke gave me a kind reminder. "Lowell, you've had a good college preparation at PUC. You also just finished the seminary program at Andrews. God has equipped and prepared you for whatever you will be called to do. Never forget that!"

Pastor Clarke was a marvelous mentor. "I'm going to include you in everything I do so you can feel comfortable in every aspect of ministry." He treated me both as a father and as an equal at the same time. I couldn't have wished for a more wonderful introduction to ministry!

Hospital visits, school worships, Pathfinders, Wednesday night prayer meeting, Friday night choir practice, preaching twice a month at the small church in Nebraska City fifty miles away, leading out there in a pilot Gift Bible program with Union College students, preaching once a month in Omaha, visiting church members, giving Bible studies made for a very busy, yet joy-filled week for me.

Another person that was a major mentor to me was Dr. Glantz, chair of the building committee. He became our much-needed dentist. Omaha Memorial had a new church building and was striving to pay off the mortgage. Every fall they had a stewardship emphasis weekend followed by church officer teams visiting every family asking for commitments to the church budget and the building fund. Dr. Glantz chose me as his visitation partner. Before the teams began to visit, they were asked to fill out personal pledge cards. Dr. Glantz kindly explained that visitors needed to experience that faith step in preparation for asking others to do the same. Carroll and I talked it over. We were both in new jobs. We had no savings. We both had college loans. We were barely making it financially, but we decided to commit $50 a month. Soon afterwards, Carroll got an unexpected raise of $50 a month.

At the conclusion of the stewardship canvass, the Omaha church held an evening fellowship meal at which members shared personal testimonies of God's special blessings in their lives during the previous year. It was a powerful evening, and we had our own miracle to share!

Dr. Glantz also introduced me to a world of potential influence outside of the Seventh-day Adventist Church. He got tickets and took me to the Governor's Prayer Breakfast in Lincoln, Nebraska. It was amazing to hear a prominent governor, Mark Hatfield of Oregon, share about how his Christian faith affected the decisions in his life in the political world!

Another very precious Omaha blessing was the extra mentoring we received from retired Pastor and Mrs. Hickman. Elder Hickman was a kindly coach in many ways, sharing from his wealth of experience. One special gift was the voice lessons and coaching that he freely offered.

Looking back, I could see how God had led in a "thousand ways," directing, equipping, and providing for all our needs. Indeed, "All His biddings are enablings" (*Christ's Object Lessons*, p. 333).

14.
STEPPING INTO PASTORAL LIFE-2

It's Sabbath morning. We're traveling south of Omaha on Highway 75 to spend our first Sabbath with the folk at the small Nebraska City church. The countryside passes rapidly, with rolling hills and bluffs overlooking the Missouri River as we cross the Platt River Basin past the Morton Salt Mansion where the celebration of Arbor Day began.

Finally, after about an hour of travel, we reach Nebraska City eager for our first glimpse of what was a little white frame church. Grass in the front yard is about a foot high! As we climb the steps, we notice broken porch floorboards with thin plywood tacked over so people wouldn't step in the holes!

We are warmly greeted by Mr. and Mrs. John Buchholz. He is the elder, and she is the Sabbath School superintendent. They are dinner hosts as well and seem to be in charge of whatever happens. The church family is made up of mostly elderly single ladies.

After church we drive to the Buchholz farm. On arriving, he says, "Hop in the pickup with me while the women lay out lunch. I need to take a quick drive around our 160 acres to check the water supply for cattle and see if they are all inside our fences."

After the drive around the farm, he stops the truck and says, "It's time for a

> *John, I didn't join this church just to be half an Adventist!*

story. When my wife and I were newlyweds, an Adventist evangelist came to town. My wife wanted to go to the meetings. We quickly got caught up in the truths presented. When the call came for baptism, we eagerly responded!

"Next came the big challenge of tithing! I said, 'I don't see how we can afford to tithe.' My wife replied, 'John, I didn't join this church just to be half an Adventist! I'm in this 100%! We can't afford NOT to tithe!' So we began returning tithe.

"That summer we had good crops. Then a terrible hailstorm came through. [We live in the middle of a hail belt.] When the storm passed, the whole area was devastated! The storm wiped out a wide path through our whole farm neighborhood—except our farm! Hail was piled up all around the fence rows of our 160 acres! Inside of our fences nothing was touched! Our crops were good! Word spread quickly! The newspaper came out and took pictures! For weeks afterwards, a train of cars came to see our 'MIRACLE FARM'!

"In the many years that have passed, yes, we have been hailed out! But God saw fit to reward the faith of a young farmer and his wife who were 'new in the faith'!"

Lunch was wonderful! Fresh cucumbers and tomatoes, green beans and corn, fresh from the garden. But better than the lunch was the story! As a fledgling new pastoral couple, we had come intending to bring blessing and encouragement to a small, struggling group, yet we were the ones who were blessed! Yes, "All God's biddings are enablings!" (*Christ's Object Lessons*, p. 333).

NEBRASKA CITY – EPILOGUE

Mr. and Mrs. Buchholz contacted the two senior young men from Union College who were serving twice a month at the Nebraska City Seventh-day Adventist Church.

Dave and Don were both super guys, dedicated and empowered with energy. Mrs. Buchholz especially glowed with this new infusion of young life into her church. It was great for their teenage son as well. We met Dave and Don soon at the quickly scheduled church business meeting on a Sunday afternoon. The church voted to fix both the front porch and the leaky roof.

Dave and Don came every other Sabbath. One would preach and the other would teach the Sabbath School lesson. After the start of the New Year of 1967, we began a pilot project for the new Gift Bible program in the Nebraska Conference. Extra students from Union College came on those weekends. Dear Sister Buchholz always provided enough food for all who came. Enough interest was generated by the evangelism students from Union College to hold a short series of meetings in April-May of that year.

15.
GREAT EXPECTATIONS

Great Expectations were in many minds as we drove up Highway 77 in route to our first church district on our own in South Sioux City, Nebraska. Fortunately, since housing was scarce, the previous pastor had put a hold on a nice, air-conditioned duplex for which we were very thankful. We met the owner, got the keys, and made arrangements for utilities.

FOR OURSELVES

We could hardly wait to meet our new church family. We were determined to love and accept them as they were. We also wanted to touch the community around us. We dropped in to meet Alice, a widowed lady living in town who was the contact person for all things church, to get some church keys. She said that the deacon was having heart trouble. Next, we drove by the church. The grass had not been mowed for several weeks. There was no plan for yard care! I was unaware that being a deacon was part of my job description! However, finding the grass that tall, I found a mower in a storage shed, mowed the lawn, and swept the sidewalk myself.

OTHER EXPECTATIONS

The conference provided a list of isolated members who expected monthly visits. In addition, all contacts from Faith for Today, It Is Written, and Voice of Prophecy came to the church mailbox.

Then there was Ingathering! That blocked out September through December. With help from members, there were ten towns where we canvassed every business during the day and then solicited every home at night. Talk about a marathon! At times Ingathering proved to be a dark cloud hanging overhead, but I discovered that the cloud did have a silver lining!

The first year, we had eleven funerals. Most were for elderly members and unchurched families whom we did not know. We accepted this as an opportunity to minister to grieving families and extend the caring mission of the church.

FOR THE PASTOR'S WIFE

There were many expectations for the pastor's wife. All families were to be visited and soon! They were spread over three counties. Of course, the pastor's wife would join in the visiting. There was no church office and no secretary. The pastor's wife was expected to cover those needs. Fortunately for me, my wife Carroll, with her English major skills, could type as fast as I could talk and then proofread and edit in the process!

Later, as we added a church bulletin and newsletter, she had to manage all those tasks with just a manual typewriter to prepare stencils for an old AB Dick monstrosity! Imagine functioning with no cell phone, no voice mail, and no computer! Yet that was reality in the 1960s! On Sabbaths, the pastoral first lady was expected to play the piano or the organ to enhance the worship services and assist with children's divisions. In just a few weeks, all the kids learned to love the pastor's wife! Hospitality and housing were other expectations. Departmental men from the conference office often stayed with us. So did the local colporteur lady. In those days, there was no plan to pay the spouse. It was expected that she was part of the pastoral package!

EXPECTATIONS FOR COMMUNITY

In some ways, Ingathering did pay off. I soon met all the business leaders of the area! The manager of our bank gladly offered his assembly room for me to have a Five-Day Plan to Stop Smoking. The complete program was on film, so I borrowed a projector from the city library. When the borrowed 16 mm projector broke down with a $75.00 repair bill, the banker himself gave a passionate speech and passed the hat!

In the spring, the Missouri River flooded the area. The National Guard imposed a curfew, closing down the town. Putting a magnetic SAWS (Seventh-day Adventist Welfare Service) sign on my car, I drove to the blockade area. The guard at the gate, recognizing me, waved me in saying, "I know you're coming to help." The need of the moment was for twenty loaves of bread, a case of mayonnaise, and several pounds of sliced ham to help the Salvation Army make ham sandwiches for the National Guard. Contacting Alice, the Dorcas lady, we went to the corner grocery. We decided to use Dorcas funds to meet the urgent need of the moment. The manager of the corner grocery sold us the food at cost. Deciding that this was not the time to have a headline in the Union Paper reading, "Adventists Fund Ham Sandwiches for the National Guard," we spent time helping the Salvation Army make dozens of sandwiches.

We arrived in rural Nebraska just as a tragic event had occurred. A Seventh-day Adventist doctor, graduate of the Guadalajara Medical School in Mexico, had come to a nearby county seat to become the only doctor in the area. He won quick fame with his skill as an amazing physician. A difficult divorce had just shattered his life. He had just disappeared, kidnapping his children and flying them to Mexico with him in his private plane! Imagine the shock and anger in town!

The Adventist Ingathering lady in the area asked me, "Do we dare do business Ingathering this year?" I responded, "Do we dare *not* go?" We sat in the banker's office as he vented! *"We really stuck out our necks to get your doctor for our town!* My bank is holding the bag for a house, a clinic, and an airplane!" I responded, "I'm sorry, sir, for this tragedy for your town—that your dream did not work out! On behalf of my church, I offer an apology. However, I want you to know that this is not representative of the work and mission of the Seventh-day Adventist Church!" The banker replied, "Thank you for having the guts to even show your face in our town!"

On canvassing another businessman near our church, he smiled, saying, "Oh, you're from the church where the walls fell down." The story went like this. Our church had been built with materials salvaged from a previous flood. After excavating for the basement, the block layers didn't brace the walls well enough. In the night the walls fell down, and the next day the walls had to be re-done! Additionally, the recycled stained-glass windows had many missing pieces, letting in dust in the summer and snow in the winter. Unfortunately, the spirit of the few remaining members matched the condition of the building!

Early in my ministry, I discovered that, when God's people begin to move in positive directions, God Himself begins to act! A strong Adventist family of six moved in, greatly strengthening the church. Then a young couple began to attend church. Being a computer tech, the husband, whose name was Harold, had to work some Friday nights. I also discovered the blessing of being part of a strong church organization. The public affairs man from the Union office joined Harold and me as we visited top officers of Iowa Beef. With the public affairs man's knowledge and diplomacy and God's intervention, Harold soon had his Sabbaths free!

In our church was an elderly, recently widowed, retired banker. His late wife, Birdie, had kept the church alive for many years. He was lonely, so I dropped by often. Upon arriving, Frank would say, "Let's go to the basement and shoot some pool." He often mentioned that Birdie wanted a more representative building for our church, and, having no children, their home was willed to the church. One day he said, "Pastor, I've got it all figured out. My days on earth are nearly over. I'm giving my house to the local church. Then we will ask the Association [the legal entity of the Conference] to buy the house for a parsonage, and you'll have money to remodel your church." I replied, "What creative thinking! I love your idea!"

That's what happened! Frank soon passed away. We found a talented remodeler who turned the old church building into a "dollhouse."

South Sioux City became the first air-conditioned Seventh-day Adventist Church in Nebraska!

With the facelift of the church, both inside and out, and with God's marvelous additions to the flock, a new day dawned for Adventists in South Sioux City!

16.
BECOMING A TEACHER MYSELF

It was Sabbath morning in Lincoln, Nebraska. I had become the new Bible teacher at College View Academy. Dennis, youth pastor for several area Seventh-day Adventist churches, had formed a "Witness Team" a few months before which often sang on Sabbaths in area churches. One of my responsibilities was to sing with the group. It was a talented group of students. Two students were accomplished ad-lib pianists. All music was memorized.

This Sabbath was extra special as we walked onto the College View Church stage to present the Sabbath School feature, for Steve, our five-year-old, was making his debut singing two children's songs. After a couple of songs by the team, Steve stepped up beside me, took his microphone, and, without missing a beat, sang his parts in "Something Special" and "Jesus, I Heard You Had A Big House." With the words, "And Jesus, I'd just like to tell you, I sure would like to go there," the sweet voice of the boy soprano ended, and there was not a dry eye in the house! The addition of children's songs became a regular feature. We sang often: at vespers, church services, weeks of prayer, and evangelistic meetings.

"Bible Labs" became an element that involved every student in College View Academy. The Witness Team was one way to serve. Academy students also ran a Neighborhood Bible Club every Sabbath afternoon. We partnered with the Good Neighbor House, an Adventist outreach for social programs in downtown Lincoln. Students ran a booth at the State Fair and assisted in the health van with screenings. We organized spring and fall clean up days when every student signed up for a community service project. These became powerful moments when students and staff served on an equal footing in community outreach helping needy people.

Two powerful occasions came on Thanksgiving Day and Christmas Day as academy students became the hands and feet and transportation help for the Good Neighbor House to prepare and deliver hot holiday meals to Lincoln's shut-in and disabled populations.

Bible Labs ensured that students learned that being a Christian was far more than giving mental assent to a certain "belief system." Being a Christian means having a caring heart and being the hands and feet of Jesus in the *here and now!*

17.

ON THE AIR IN MUNCIE, INDIANA

The year was 1978. I was the new pastor in Muncie, Indiana. The phone rang. It was Sybil Bennet, manager of the WERK radio station. She spoke convincingly in her usual rapid-fire style.

"There's a radio spot workshop coming soon at Andrews. H.M.S. Richards, Sr., is co-hosting it. I want you to go. I'll give you a free radio spot for every one that the church pays for, and I'll help you raise the money from the church. We need to do something new to break out into the community. I think you could do this."

Wow! The challenge was appealing. Shortly after this, my family and I found ourselves in Berrien Springs, Michigan, staying in the basement of a friend's place while I immersed myself in the radio-spot class co-taught by Dr. Jim Chase and H.M.S. Richards, Sr.

Radio breakthrough ministry was an exciting new idea with great appeal to me, though not without some feelings of apprehension! After the introduction into the possibilities in radio, we were given samples of thirty second spots produced by the VOP "Sonspot" team and a booklet of sixty second spots by Jim Chase of Andrews University radio, and then we were turned loose into the new WAUS station lab to get a feel for what might be a good fit for us.

Very quickly I discovered that thirty second spots were a better fit for me. They also cost less money, so I could be on the air more often.

With Sybil's enthusiastic support and Andrews' offer to freely use and adapt their copy, we were quickly up and going and on the air. The small church was very proud to have their voice on the major local station at both morning and evening "drive times."

Every Friday afternoon became the weekly time to record a week of spots. With a little experience, ideas for seasonal messages flooded my mind, and I never had a challenge to come up with new ideas.

Again, I discovered the truth of that special God-given promise, "All His biddings are enablings" (*Christ's Object Lessons*, p. 333).

18.
ATTACK ON OUR SONS

EPISODE 1

It was a bright sunny morning in July. We had just finished the remodeling of our Muncie church and were cleaning everything up, getting ready for the dedication weekend. I was high on a ladder washing the tall exterior windows. Suddenly the peace of the morning was shattered by the snarls of a dog and the screams of a child! The child being attacked by the dog was wearing red pants! Then it dawned on me—that was *my* six-year-old son bleeding on the ground! I leaped from the ladder, landed in a shrub, raced across the street to the yard where all the church kids were playing! I grabbed a swing pole from the ground, drove off the angry dog, picked up my bleeding son, and raced back to our car!

By that time, my wife, who was nine months pregnant with our third child, met me at our hatchback Ford Fiesta. She climbed into the back, held our bleeding son in her lap! We raced to Ball Memorial Hospital, which was close by. When we reached the hospital, all three of us were covered in blood! The ER tech who met us shouted, "Which one of you is it?"

When the ER team saw our son with deep gashes in the back of his head, neck and shoulders, bleeding profusely, they seemed to freeze into inaction. One of the nurses called our family doctor, discovering that he was right there, making his morning rounds. When he appeared shortly with a plastic surgeon in tow, the ER exploded into action! They poured a saline solution over David's head, getting him ready to immediately go to surgery!

As you can imagine, this proved to be a traumatic moment for Carroll and me and for a little guy in shock! But we could be grateful for several things: our trusted doctor and a plastic surgeon were immediately present; the dog was known and chained up—important for possible rabies issues; we were grateful that our son had fallen face forward, so wounds were on the back of his head and not on his face; and we knew that a loving God was very present and just as concerned as we were!

> In the middle of the night, David said, "Daddy, can you rub my left hand?"

The first night in the hospital was tough. With stitches and bandages on the back of David's head, he had to lie on his stomach and side. Both the shock and the pain were intense! He had IVs in his right hand. In the middle of the night, David said, "Daddy, can you rub my left hand?"

It was then that a sudden realization hit me. In another time and another place, there was another Father and another Son who suffered. Only in that case, the Father could not be present with His Son. His presence was hidden. The Son had to deal with the intense pain and suffering all alone! In a flash, I understood how much the Father loved His Son, how much the Father loved us, and how much both the Father and the Son had given for our redemption!

EPISODE 2

About a month after David's dog bite episode, we had another dog bite event. Muncie was a three-church district, so I always had an early church in another place. School had started, and our bussed students needed to go to the Anderson Church to sing. The lady who owned the dog was transporting Muncie students in her station wagon. Steve, who was carefully avoiding the dog yard, needed to get into the car's right back door. As he was getting into the car, the dog rushed to the end of its chain, grabbed Steve's arm, tearing up his suitcoat sleeve, and gave Steve's arm several bites. Carroll borrowed a car, got Steve treated at the ER before I arrived from the early church service. (This was before cell phones.) She instructed the elders not to say a word about the episode as it might make me too upset to preach.

I arrived at Muncie during the opening hymn. As I glanced over the congregation, I was stunned to see Steve there, dressed in a T-shirt with a bandaged arm, sitting by his mom. The minute church was over, the story exploded! I quickly called the owner of the dog and the elders and deacons for an immediate intervention meeting. It wasn't easy as I had already had a similar meeting with the dog owners a month before just after David's severe dog bite attack. This time I involved church leaders and stated that I would do another police report that very day. We ended up having to take legal action.

Then, right in the middle of this mess, we got the sudden call to teach in California. The story hasn't ended yet, but we did end up taking the teaching job in California.

The first night in California, Steve woke us in the middle of the night clutching his throat unable to breathe. Steve had had a tetanus shot in Muncie. He was having a severe allergic reaction! Nothing surprises God. In the midst of our uncertainty God had all the answers ready. First, we were not on the road. We had arrived at our destination in California. The first night in our new place, we stayed with our friends the Gramliches. The wife of another teacher, Lavon Turner, was a nurse who worked at Alta Hospital. The chief of staff was Dr. Will Wonderly, an Adventist doctor. We received immediate, quality medical care in the middle of the night just when we urgently needed it. We had instant resources made available to direct us through this potential disaster! God is good. Once again, we realized that nothing is unknown to God. "All His biddings are enablings" (*Christ's Object Lessons*, p. 333).

19.
DEODORA MEMORIES

It was Sunday of Labor Day weekend. My friend, Sam Gramlich, from Dinuba, California, was on the phone.

"Have you ever considered teaching again? I need a grade 7-10 teacher immediately that is certified for junior academy Bible, history, and English. P.E. and music are covered by others."

I was pastoring the three churches of the Muncie, Indiana, district. We were at a possible transition point. The Muncie Church had just been remodeled and dedicated. We had just completed a successful series of meetings. Our two older boys, grades 1 and 4, faced lengthy bussing to get to school. My wife, Carroll, desired a less demanding role in order to be a stay-at-home mom with our two-month-old third son. We decided that I should fly to California for an interview.

Fortunately, as scheduling was tight, I wore a suit for the flight. That was a good thing since my luggage got lost and it arrived by taxi just as I was leaving for my return flight home.

The interview went well with the board voting to hire me that night. We put up a for sale by owner sign and our house sold on the second day. We greatly diminished our belongings by a successful yard sale. And then it was, "California, here we come!"

Sam Gramlich, my new principal, accurately briefed me on the realities of the situation. I would face both academic and behavioral challenges. However, having worked with Sam before, I knew that I would have the principal's backing. He counseled me to be firm with discipline from the beginning and set high academic expectations.

I'd been forewarned that I would soon be tested by some unruly students. It happened the very first morning! A local area pastor's wife, Kathy Lockwood, made a successful beginning to the school year as a substitute teacher. Students had the habit of kneeling and participating in the morning prayer time. As I was ready to say the closing prayer, I sensed a slight disturbance in the back corner. Two boys with raised hands threw oranges at the front blackboard! As we arose, I addressed them by name, telling them to remain with me in the room for lunch. They could not eat outside at the picnic tables.

"Mr. Dunston, don't you know that you're supposed to close your eyes during prayer? How did you see us?" I replied, "Well, *you* obviously didn't close *your* eyes! Besides, there's a special verse in the Bible possibly written just for teachers, 'Watch and pray!' The first law of learning is cooperation and respect. I'm calling your parents. You will be suspended from school tomorrow!" A few days later, I was tested again.

John, who was sixteen, drove himself to school in an aging pickup, leaving early at the last period study hall to go to a job.

Still being hot in September, classroom doors were wide open, and ours was very close to the parking lot. As John prepared to leave, another boy slipped out, popped the hood of John's truck, and jerked a spark plug wire loose. It wasn't hard to put two and two together. So another boy got a well-deserved suspension. A few weeks later, a fight (both verbal and physical) erupted in P.E. Several boys earned three-day suspensions—some being school leaders. After that, things began to settle down.

We also faced some immediate academic challenges. About half of the ninth-tenth grade class was made up of students with English as a second language. The English texts on hand were for transformational grammar (a specialized text). Most students didn't have a clue about what was going on in English class. I told the principal that I could not teach from that text! Sam, a specialist in reading-language arts, put in a rush order for a traditional English text. With it we made rapid progress. But then we faced another challenge. I soon discovered that three ninth-grade boys could not read! Resourceful Sam took them out of regular English class, and, by using a novel reading approach (audio-visual-tactile), he had them reading and back in regular English class in one semester. (Incidentally, four years later, all three boys graduated from Monterey Bay Academy.)

ACTIONS SPEAK LOUDER THAN WORDS

After a challenging beginning, we had three happy and rewarding years at Dinuba Junior Academy. I greatly enjoyed my years being a teaching colleague with Sam Gramlich. We made a good team. He was one of the most knowledgeable and authentic people I ever worked with.

The Central California Conference had some exciting summer plans to reach out and touch communities. With six of our outstanding upper graders, we received a grant to operate a summer day camp. The students planned chapels, crafts, sports activities, and even lunch, and they received scholarships for academy. I only had to supervise!

Principal Sam Gramlich kicked off each school year with a special bonding event for grades 7–10—a much looked forward to backpack trip into California high country. One morning in the fall of 1981, two bears invaded camp. *Bear-experienced* Mr. Lewis ran yelling and arm-waving, and the bears ran crashing through the brush! Students now believed the teacher's advice to hoist all food securely in back packs attached to cables pulled high off the ground! Cooperation, personal responsibility, wilderness survival, group bonding, and hearing God's voice in His second book of nature were all accomplished in this three-day trip.

Another special Deodora memory were the staff potluck dinner occasions, which created staff bonding and unity. Marlene Gramlich and her famous enchiladas always held center place.

Summers in the San Joaquin Valley were extremely hot. Fortunately, Dinuba had early church at 8:30 followed by Sabbath School. Families with children pooled potluck food and fled to the coolness of Kings Canyon and Sequoia National Parks only an hour away. We spent many a happy Sabbath with the Baerg, Escobar, Gramlich, Markham, Sage, and Turner families (mostly Dinuba and Sierra View teachers).

At first, I thought that *Deodora Memories* was a strange name for a school yearbook. Recently I took a walk back through nostalgia, looking through all my Dinuba year books with that name. That triggered many happy memories: the large Deodora spruce that shaded my classroom, happy faces of my old students and their antics, their amazing academic growth and progress, supportive parents gratefully bringing teachers many boxes of citrus fruit and avocados, warm staff relationships—several now awaiting the call of the Lifegiver and entrance to a Better Land. That's a major part of what Adventist Education prepares us for!

20.
RICHLAND OUTREACH

Our family had just arrived in a new pastorate. Richland Church leaders met to brainstorm about priorities in ministry. Three things rose to the top: spiritual growth of members, social fellowship needs (members were scattered geographically), and touching the community around us.

For spiritual growth and fellowship needs, the church chose to focus on Growth Groups. Host Homes were offered. Group leaders and teachers were chosen. Each group chose its own curriculum. A special asset were sisters-in-law Cindy and Judy, as both had backgrounds in Bible Study Fellowship. They created an impressive library of inductive Books of the Bible study lessons. Several elders conducted Daniel-Revelation seminars for outreach. These groups brought friends, neighbors, and spouses into the church at a comfortable pace.

A special community outreach took place in Benton City. Following a Bible seminar outreach, a Vacation Bible School took place at the local elementary school. While it was a very successful event, the finale was unforgettable! The concluding evening was oppressively hot, the ladies planned a glorious outdoor reception for the significant audience of children, parents, and guests. The graduation event had just concluded! Refreshments were set out on tables on the lawn! Then—surprise! Unbeknown to all of us helpers, underground sprinklers raised their giant ugly heads at 8:30 p.m. Instantly several VBS workers had the presence of mind to jump on top of a sprinkler head to save the guests from cold showers! Luckily a local person quickly found the custodian to shut the shower down!

We reached out to the surrounding community in other ways. When I mentioned doing radio spots to reach a new audience and that I'd had some previous experience, the idea caught the interest of church officers. John, a new member and new personal ministries leader, offered to lead in a demographic survey.

We settled on a new radio station with a targeted listening audience of ages eighteen to forty-five. The station was fast-growing, holding second place in the area. At the initial visit, the management was open to recording church spots but was cautious about a local pastor doing the recording and wanted their DJs to do the honors to save studio time by not having a novice waste time doing retakes. After explaining that I had previous radio spot experience, they agreed to allow a trial time.

While it was exciting to have another opportunity to go on the air, the expectations added extra pressure. The mission was laced with prayer and careful preparation for the weekly recording sessions. Spots were carefully written, with timed practice readings to ensure good flow, and they were clipped to fit the station's twenty-six-second time slots.

Driving to the first recording session, I was filled with feelings of euphoria! The session went well. I recorded five spots to be played at morning and evening drive times. We did not have to do any retakes. This became a weekly pattern and one of my most looked forward to moments of the week.

The church family supported the new outreach and looked forward to crisp devotional thoughts each day. One day when I came in to record, the station manager asked to speak with me at the end of the session. I wondered, *What is coming? Have I done something egregious?* He began by complimenting me for the quality of the content of the radio spots, then he smilingly asked, "Do you know the nickname the DJs have given you?"

"No," I responded.

He then said, "You are known as 'The one take wonder.' " (Thank You, Lord!)

Again, I remembered that favorite Ellen White quotation of mine, "All His biddings are enablings" (*Christ's Object Lessons*, p. 333).

21.
WASHINGTON D.C., HERE WE COME!

The idea for a D.C. trip for ninth-graders was born at Rosario on a graduation trip for twelve eighth-graders from Central Valley Junior Academy in 1994. Mike and June Miner joined principal Lowell and my wife as chaperones.

We experienced so much fun that we envisioned more! So Washington, D.C., here we come! Mike, knowing D.C. personally from military days, became chief logician.

A much-needed document for school tour entrance was secret service approval. Mike got that in hand by February, but alas, no reply came from our Senator's office in Spokane for the desired White House tour passes!

WASHINGTON D.C., HERE WE COME!

We would need to raise about $1,000 a month. Our first target was a fall yard sale. An amazing amount of stuff poured in netting around $1500.00. We were ecstatic! Students rose to the occasion selling scissors and hundreds of boxes of chocolates. Parents and churches rallied to support. Next, a Christmas bazaar netted a major amount. Supportive parent and main teacher sub, Sharon Waymire, collected recipes and edited a popular cookbook (that is still in use). With another yard sale in springtime, along with continued student selling, by April the magic goal of $8,000 was in hand, and we were on our way!

We hit D.C. at peak cherry blossom time along with hundreds of others on spring break! Long lines—so what? While waiting in line at the Washington Monument, we got to view the Clinton motorcade close-up. Our tour group was blessed in many ways. We connected with a Seventh-day Adventist tour guide from Montana who'd grown up in the D.C. area and who was visiting her dad. She put us in touch with a Montana Senate page who gave us a privileged tour of the Senate, even with a ride on the new underground train for senators. On returning from the Senate tour, an impromptu idea hit us—why not crash Senator Gordan's office and ask why we did not get the requested White House tour passes? On arriving with our fourteen-strong delegation, I asked to speak with the senior office person there. At that moment, I sensed a "presence" right behind me. Noelle spoke up: "We're from a school in Washington state. We may be small, but we're just as important as anyone else. We students worked for a year to raise money for this trip. We have Secret Service clearance. The thing I looked forward to the most was to tour the White House, and we didn't even hear back from your office." (It wasn't lost on the lady that Noelle was both a woman and a person of color.)

Our attendant was immediately shaken. Office personnel, obviously flustered, began looking frantically through drawers. They came up with only three passes, holding them out to us. Noelle spoke up again, "If we can't all go, no one will go!"

As a group, we turned and left. Though we did not acquire what we desired, we were all proud of Noelle. We also felt proud that our class had given some Washington bureaucrats a dose of realism that day, hoping that our encounter might open the door to fairer treatment to small schools in the future. Some sobering moments awaited us: the Holocaust Museum and the Vietnam Wall. When Michael J. Miner found his very name engraved there, the finality of war hit us all! (Obviously, there had been another "Michael J. Miner.")

For weekend activities we rented two vans. Thursday, we toured Jefferson's Monticello home. We were amazed at both his gardens and his inventions. On Sabbath, our guide arranged the trade of a Sabbath School feature for a potluck dinner at the Manassas church where she grew up. We visited Civil War battlefield sights in the afternoon.

This Washington, D.C., trip proved to be one of the highlights of my total teaching career!

Wonderful human interactions between teacher and students, experiencing Americana in a way impossible from media and books, sharing this experience with my wife, youngest son, and life-long friends was a momentous learning event rich with many warm memories!

We toured many places: Arlington National Cemetery, the Tomb of the Unknown Soldier, the Supreme Court, the Lincoln Memorial, Ford's Theater, several days at the Smithsonian, and the Holocaust Museum.

22.

GOD'S SCHOOL

School was just over for the day. My cell phone was ringing.

"Hello, this is Ray Geigle. Remember me?"

"Yes, I do."

"Can you come up to Providence Hospital in Everett as soon as possible? Dad is experiencing kidney failure and wants to talk with the Cypress School principal."

"I can make it by 4:00, OK?"

We had become acquainted with Ray and Etta Geigle. As head deacon and deaconess of Mt. Tabor Seventh-day Adventist Church in Portland, Oregon, they had presided over several funeral dinners for my wife's aging family members. Ray had grown up at the old

Mountlake Terrace School-Edmonds area; and Etta, at the old Ballard Church and Seattle Jr. Academy.

When I entered the hospital room, Ray introduced me to his dad, Reuben, and his two brothers. Reuben asked his sons to go to supper and give him an hour with the Cypress principal.

> "Mr. Dunston, are you aware that you are principal of God's School, a real miracle school?"

"Mr. Dunston, are you aware that you are principal of God's School, a real miracle school? I don't have long to live, and I want you to hear from my lips just how we got God's School." In the next few minutes the following story spilled out.

Reuben had worked many years in the custodial department of the Edmonds School District. The superintendent told him one day that the Cypress property, then used for storage, would soon go up for auction. He continued, "I know that you Adventists run schools, and I'd like for your people to have a chance at this."

At that very time, the Edmonds church had discussed an expansion project for additional classrooms and a gym at the Mountlake Terrace School for around $600,000. A meeting of the area Adventist churches was called.

The Cypress property had twenty classrooms, library-office, gym-kitchen, all on ten secluded acres available for less money (about $390,000). Those men and women of great vision voted to move out in faith and purchase the Cypress property.

Pastor Roger Ferris, of Volunteer Park, and Pastor Don Scully, of Edmonds, were asked to deliver the bid the next morning. After special prayer together, the pastors felt strongly impressed to raise the bid by $5,000. Had they not raised the bid, the Cypress property would have gone to another bidder.

Another providential event solved the down payment problem. On overhearing an Adventist discussion about the Cypress miracle, a lady of another Christian entity looking for a property reported that the Mountlake Terrace School might be for sale, which led to a quick cash sale providing the down payment money for the Cypress property.

Here we come to an interesting wrinkle in the story reported to me in one of my last visits with Pastor Ferris. Since the pastors raised the bid on their own, without waiting for group support, they were held responsible to come up with the extra $5,000. On inspecting the Cypress plant, they discovered thousands of old textbooks in mothballs. Resourceful Pastor Roger and friends from Volunteer Park rented a truck, hauling many loads of books to a recycler raising the additional five grand.

I feel very blessed indeed to have known some of the "faith heroes" from the archives of the Cypress past and to have heard these precious memories from their lips.

FOLLOWING ARE SOME THE HEROES OF HEBREWS 11 (Cypress Version):

Reuben Geigle

Roger and Ida Ferris

Wilbur and Sara Howell

Dorothea Searson

23.
PUGET SOUND ADVENTURES

It happened on a spring morning in March of 1996. I left the Yakima Valley early, heading to Seattle for an interview for the position of principal at Cypress Adventist School. A cacophony of thoughts raced through my mind as the miles sped away. Did I want to move to the city? Would this move be good for me, for my wife, and for my family? I would be assuming two positions—a full time 7-8 grade teacher and principalship of a larger school. Could I handle it? Would it be fulfilling? Where did God want me to serve?

When I arrived, I was pleasantly surprised to find the school was in a country location on ten acres surrounded by woods and mature subdivisions. It did not feel like a big city. When I walked in, the first feeling of the available board members was warm and pleasant. The chairwoman introduced me to those seated around the table. Donna, a Green Lake member, was a choir friend of my niece who taught music and was taking graduate work at the University of Washington. I had taken classes at Andrews with Pastor Glen's brother and cousin. Pastor Larry and I remembered each other from Dr. Running's Hebrew class, also at Andrews University. Pastor Joe warmly shared that his daughter taught in a school where my brother was the principal. He stated that he was an excellent leader. He further commented that he felt that good things ran in families and was very happy for me to come and interview.

The board chair was flabbergasted. At the conclusion of these introductions, she commented, "It's not fair! I didn't grow up Adventist!" An additional plus was that the director of education, David Escobar, was a former college classmate of mine, a seasoned educational leader, known as a strong supporter of teachers. The interview went well.

Pastor Joe took me to lunch. He further described both the needs and challenges of the potential job. He strongly urged me to consider it and said that he felt that I embodied in experience what they were looking for in a principal to lead Cypress Adventist School into the future.

Later in the afternoon, I enjoyed meeting the members of the school staff. They seemed like a mature group of teachers. The Adventist schools in the area were facing change and restructuring with the new day academy coming to Kirkland. It felt like a chance for me to grow and to provide leadership into a new era and bring stability to a good school situation.

A few days later the "official call came through, and we accepted it in faith, believing that "All His biddings are enablings" (*Christ's Object Lessons*, p. 333).

24.
CYPRESS MONEY CHALLENGES AND MIRACLES

Soon after arriving at Cypress Adventist School, I was faced with two money challenges: scholarship funds and re-doing seven roofs. Eileen, the school secretary and treasurer, had kept meticulous financial records. The plan in 1996 was to take a small amount of church subsidy for the scholarship fund. However, the need for more funds quickly grew!

Every August, Eileen would say, "Lowell, write your best letter." We would send out letters to everyone who had ever donated to Cypress, include a return envelope, and, with prayer, place the letters in the mail. Donations, large and small, would trickle in.

Miracles did happen! Having five constituent churches, I became a circuit-riding principal, visiting and often preaching around my route. Just before Christmas we had registration for the second semester. I needed about $8,000 more right away for scholarships. Only treasurer Eileen and I knew. Now it was the last Sabbath in the year. I had planned to visit a certain church. As I got into my car, I had a strong impression to go in a different direction. I abruptly changed my plans and went to another church. After services were over, someone approached me saying, "Lowell, could you use some money?" I responded, "Yes, my school always needs scholarship money." A check was written, folded, and handed to me. When I got into my car, I expectantly unfolded it. Amazing! It was for $10,000!

We soon would have a new opportunity and a new challenge. Fannie Ulsch, retired high school Spanish teacher, had raised up a new Hispanic company which had many young families. She came to visit me sharing her dream of providing an Adventist education for those children, many of whom were new in the faith. I agreed. We visited the conference office sharing her vision with the Hispanic coordinator and his wife. They were excited about her vision but had no money resources for schools.

We had found a donor to buy a set of tone-chimes for our music program. Fannie invited us to bring our chime and vocal choirs to her church. I would preach. She would translate.

At the end of worship, she made a call for all who were interested in having an Adventist education to come forward. A large group surged to the front! Positive Adventist students have a powerful magnetic draw!

One day I had a strong compulsion to take our concern for Hispanic scholarship funds up a notch with the Union. I poured out my feelings in a strong letter and sent copies to the NPUC officers. Shortly afterwards, I was invited to attend the yearly NPUC education council in Portland. Elementary delegates came mid-morning. Secondary people had their meetings first.

Early on the agenda was a discussion about the need for Hispanic scholarship funds. The treasurer stated that, as the committee convened to discuss items for the education summit agenda, a strong letter from Lowell had arrived. He said that the letter vividly laid out the key points for a much-needed Hispanic scholarship fund, that there was growing interest in the NPUC on this issue, and that my letter served as a catalyst for discussion as it summarized the main points of the issue:

1. The major growth factor in NPUC was in the accessions to Hispanic membership.
2. The Hispanic churches had large numbers of children and youth.
3. These youth—many new in the faith—urgently needed the opportunity of an Adventist education, maybe more than others.
4. Since the church was evangelizing this community, we had a moral obligation to provide them with the opportunity to obtain an Adventist education.
5. The church has an open door of opportunity here. We need to step up and do something NOW!

Imagine how excited we were when a few months later the NPUC announced plans for a new Hispanic Scholarship Fund! It would provide funding for 100 students yearly in the NPUC through a four-way plan that would include the NPUC, local conference, local church, and the family—each entity providing for one-fourth of the tuition. What a miracle! One of the most exciting things in being an Adventist worker is to be used by God as an instrument in His work!

ANOTHER MIRACLE!

At Cypress Adventist School we needed a $40,000 roof repair immediately. We also needed more scholarship funds. Often in staff meetings we brought school needs to the Lord in prayer. One day, as Eileen, the secretary, opened the mail, she stepped through my open door saying, "Are you sitting down? Look at this!" In shaky handwriting was this note, "Here's a check in memory of my late wife. Use the money as you see fit." Inside was a check for $82,000. Again, we thought that only our office knew of these urgent needs of the moment. Sometimes we need to be reminded that Someone up above knows all about our needs. We are only earthly agents in His hands! (Isn't God *good?*)

Of course we sent a thank you note. There was a return address. However, in checking with many old-timers, no one had ever heard of this man! We could never trace who he was!

After being at Cypress School for over a decade, one spring the custodian informed me that the riding mower that had served us for over twenty years was dying. Cypress sat on ten acres and mowing season had just begun. The facilities committee presented the need to the board, recommending that we ask for an $8,000 loan from the NPUC Revolving Fund. The motion passed. After adjournment, a board member approached me saying, "Don't you borrow that money! Keep this under your hat, but I just came into a significant sum of money. I want to buy the school a new mower—not a cheap one, but a good one that will last!" Rick Roberts and I went to the tractor centers in Monroe. We settled on the Cub Cadet as the best buy. When we talked about payment, the sales rep referred us to the owner. He replied, "You probably don't know this, but we are an Adventist business, so as a church entity you are entitled to a major discount. I recommend that you upgrade to a top-of-the-line machine. It will better meet your needs." (Thank you, Lord!)

For nineteen years as Cypress principal, it was my challenge and privilege to provide access to an Adventist Christian education both to those within Adventism and to those "other-sheep from other-folds" who desired what we offered. Maybe because of my own challenges to receive such an education, I committed *never* to turn away a parent or a student lacking financial resources who desired a Christian education such as we offered. Over the years, gifts—both large and small—poured into the Cypress special funds. I'm eternally grateful that many of our constituent members also caught the vision of how such an education could prepare our students for service to God and mankind—both for the here and now and in the hereafter (see *Education*, p. 19). God abundantly blessed our faith and our efforts. Over those two decades, around half a million dollars came in for the Cypress Adventist School scholarship fund and other special projects. "ALL HIS BIDDINGS ARE ENABLINGS" (*Christ's Object Lessons*, p. 333).

25.
JACK AND JILL MUST HAVE PLAY

"All work and no play indeed do make Jack and Jill dull boys and girls!" A major crisis hit the children of Cypress School in the spring of 1997. The much-loved center of recess fun: the gigantic wooden "Big Toy" began giving up the ghost piece by piece. Northwest weather had taken its toll! Caution tape soon engulfed the complete creature in mothballs! It was rendered useless!

Two men hastened to the rescue. Rick Roberts, our teacher-custodian, quickly researched all types of playground equipment. Dan Booher, board member, created an action plan to get things moving. Word of the special need spread quickly. Money came rolling in. As a foreman at Mehrer Drywall, Dan elicited Don Mehrer's help.

Sunday work bees brought both the Mehrer crew and equipment plus Cypress volunteers. First, the demolition crew took action! After a minimal time of taking things apart, old posts—set in cement—had to be lifted by hydraulic action. Since all wood had been treated, it was considered toxic waste to be hauled away and properly disposed of.

After a leveling of the land, Dan and Rick measured the area, driving stakes in readiness for the next volunteer crew to construct the new "Big Toy." This one, made of steel and vinyl, would be indestructible (or so we thought).

It was a gorgeous "Big Toy" *BEAST*, with red steel posts, red monkey bars, red walkway, yellow climbing wall, yellow umbrella top, blue straight slide, green curving slide—a major source of pride to all who saw it: students, teachers, parents, and constituents—and on weekends neighborhood friends—parents and kids alike. Two sets of swings were soon added.

"Jack and Jill" experienced many happy hours of enjoyment playing there! In addition, teachers shared in the recess joy—blessed by the endorphin-enriched brains of happy red-faced students on their return from recess.

But alas! The *indestructible became destructible!* All it took was a crazed, insane pyromaniac, late on the night of the Fourth of July, to torch ours and several other playgrounds in the area—just to see multicolored flames shoot fifty feet high for a few fleeting minutes!

But—thank God—our cloud of depression contained a silver lining!

As Mrs. Richmond, our secretary, and Mr. Roberts, our custodian, examined our insurance policy, it included both the "Big Toy" itself and free installation of a replacement. *HALLELUJAH!*

If one carefully examines the red posts, they might still detect some faint marks of fire—reminders that God indeed still does look after His own and that "Jack and Jill" still need play in order to return to class with endorphin-enriched brains ready to learn again.

26.
KEEP THOSE SCHOOL VANS GOING

"OLD BLUE" MIRACLE VAN 1

It was the summer of 1997, my second year as the Cypress principal. Dr. Gruesbeck, retired pastor of Green Lake Church, had assumed the shepherd role of the Ballard flock. He called one day stating that he had six students for Cypress from Ballard. He had a van driver ready. All we needed was a bus.

The Volunteer Park Seventh-day Adventist Church stepped up to the plate. They had run a bus for about twenty years bringing Seattle kids to Cypress. Their old, blue Ford bus was in "moth balls." While "Old Blue" was faded on the outside, she was still mechanically sound on the inside. They offered to give the bus to Cypress. Wow! We were up and going. The Ballard six soon mushroomed to a full load of fifteen passengers.

"Old Blue" and driver James provided about five years of faithful service before "Old Blue" "gave up the ghost."

THE GREEN DODGE, MIRACLE VAN 2

We were into another search for a van. The best buy that we found was a two-tone green Dodge fifteen-passenger van in good condition listed for $6,995. We had about $6,000 on hand. When we arranged to pick up the vehicle, the owner said, "When we discovered that Cypress School was the buyer, we reduced the price to $6,000. Our kids have been in Little League for several summers using your ball fields. You have been generous to the community. We want to give something back to you." (THANK YOU, LORD!)

The Green Dodge provided several years of good service before a multitude of challenges came unexpectedly again.

A CHALLENGING INTERLUDE

Van challenges, such as a breakdown or a driver illness, were covered by the Dunstons' and Roberts' mini vans always waiting in readiness. We were called upon for a quick rescue several times. Then came the bombshell! Suddenly, James was no longer available to drive! What could we do?

I suddenly became the morning driver, leaving early in order for the kids to reach school by 8:20 a.m., and Mr. Roberts did the afternoon driving shift. Thirty-five miles through city traffic at rush hour times made up the route. Rather than a drag, however, the morning trek became enjoyable with cheerful student greetings as they climbed into the van, happy singing of songs learned in music class and Friday chapels, and the daily chant of riders shouting, "Mr. D., there's your church," as the bus rolled past St. Dunston's Episcopal every day, and the "Thank you, Mr. D.," as students, grateful for the opportunity of a Christian education, disembarked. Seven weeks rolled by until an unemployed dad took over the driving, and I sort of missed those morning moments with those special few.

> *The morning trek became enjoyable with cheerful student greetings as they climbed into the van, happy singing of songs learned in music class and Friday chapels.*

THE WHITE DODGE- MIRACLE VAN-3

When we needed a new van driver, the good Lord brought us Mr. Ted to be both van driver and custodian. When we hired Ted, we also unknowingly found a needed P.E. teacher (due to his years as a Boy Scout leader). After Ted took over, we suddenly faced a new van challenge. Due to nationwide accidents, our insurance carrier would no longer insure fifteen-passenger vehicles. All summer long our search for another van went nowhere. Then one day the music teacher saw a notice that Community Transit was offering a chance for non-profits to participate in a drawing for a limited number of vehicles. Ted and I rushed in an application, barely making the deadline.

The day that Ted, my wife, and I went to the drawing was a big moment of suspense! In the random drawing of a straw from a cup, we drew a twelve-passenger white Dodge van in mint condition, the best of the lot (again, we thank our great God)! All for FREE! *The impossible became the possible once again due to God's amazing intervention!* The *keynote* of my life proved true once again: "All His biddings are enablings" (*Christ's Object Lessons*, p. 333).

27.
THE CYPRESS PAINT PARTY

Being a painting contractor was not on my resume, but that became my role the summer of 2007. The Cypress board had discussed the need to repaint the school exterior for some time, but how to find the personnel and how to pay for repainting of four large buildings were unanswered questions.

The project was launched unexpectedly by a phone call from Fannie Ulsch, a Cypress board member and an apostle to the Washington Conference Hispanic work. She was also a translator for Northwest SAGE (Seniors in Action for God with Excellence) projects in Spanish speaking countries. "Lowell, a SAGE project just fell through. If you can act fast and be ready in three weeks, I can have at least twenty-five people to help paint Cypress School. Bob Grady, the SAGE manager, is looking for another project close to home.

Word spread quickly. Roger Ferris called, "I hear that SAGE may paint Cypress School. Don't spend a penny on paint. You know that in my retirement I manage the warehouses at Auburn Academy. We just had a client die. I'm left with a whole warehouse full of paint to dispose of. How soon could you and Rick Roberts come down?"

When Rick and I arrived at AAA (Auburn Adventist Academy), Roger had Mrs. Kirkman at the warehouse. We climbed over many skids of paint, finally finding many five-gallon pails of sage green and more pails of tan. Mr. and Mrs. Kirkman, famous Adventist architects, felt that the sage green and tan combination would be great earthtones for our buildings.

There were more hurdles to conquer! The tilted-up white rock walls were covered with the dust of the ages. For paint to stick, the walls must be power washed and dry for a few days. A man temporarily in the area called, "I'm a retired school board chair. I know how hard it is to get volunteers. Would it help if I came next week with my power washer?" (Would it ever!)

Then Teresa Jones called. "Could I send Matthew and Conner to help you next week?" (By all means!) They were two great, dependable boys! Mr. Ted loaned his power washer. With a volunteer and me power washing from ladders and the Jones boys power washing from the ground, all the walls got washed and had the weekend to dry before the Monday painting was to begin.

Another detail remained. What about all the equipment we would need for the volunteers? Contractor, Martin Bode called, offering to prepare the needed list and take me around to paint stores on Friday to accomplish this much needed task. We had Sunday left to lay everything out on the gym floor and get organized. Teacher Roberts, a former painting contractor, took care of another complex detail. Different paint had to be used for the metal doors and frames.

A final detail was answered by the ladies of the Cypress Staff: breakfast and lunch needed to be arranged for the volunteers.

When Fannie Ulsch called, my first thought was, *Would I be fool hardy to take on such a huge project on such short notice? How could we plan for and accomplish all the necessary preparatory steps and be ready in three weeks?* Some Old Testament stories provided some great encouragement. For the Israelites in the time of Moses to have a path through the Red Sea, Moses had to stretch out his hand (Exod. 14:21). For a second generation of Israelites, in the time of Joshua, to cross the Jordan River at flood stage, the priests had to step into the waters of the Jordan (Joshua 3:15). A "faith walk" requires leaders to risk putting their feet into the water! Hindsight shows that, before we even knew what to ask for, God had all the answers ready ahead of time. God impressed people to call us with the ready-made solutions for every piece of the paint-party puzzle—even the perfect time-sequencing of every needed process in the proper order!

Monday morning dawned, thirty-five SAGE volunteers showed up, and we were ready! Two more special blessings materialized! First, many of the SAGE folk were among the Cypress founders (bringing back many precious memories)!

Second, one of the SAGE recruits was a commercial spray-painter from the Oregon SAGE group. He was fast and competent, enabling us to finish our gigantic task in just one week!

Friday, as I reviewed how all the pieces of Cypress Paint Party puzzle fit together, I was amazed! Once again, I was reminded that with God, "All things are possible!" The *impossible can become possible*, but for miracles to happen, we must first be willing to put our feet into the water!

And I was reminded once again that INDEED, "ALL HIS BIDDINGS ARE ENABLINGS"

(*Christ's Object Lessons*, p. 333).

28.
IT'S A SMALL WORLD

"It's A Small World," at least in Adventist circles!

We were heading north on I-5 toward Walla Walla University's Rosario Station, a research facility at Rosario Beach in Washington State, for a three-day Science Camp. For Cypress Adventist schoolers, grades 5-8, this was the most-looked-forward-to moment of the school year—three glorious days at Rosario!

Four seven-passenger vans were full of happy, expectant campers ready to plunge into three days of action-packed marine biology adventures. Andrew Rice, contract biologist, would be waiting ready to begin class on our arrival.

My co-pilot in the front of my Dodge Caravan was David, a new boy in the 6th grade. Being a talkative kid, he was telling me about just visiting his grandparents, who live in a very remote area of northeast Oregon. As he continued talking, things began to sound familiar. Suddenly it clicked! I had visited with his grandfather at a PUC Prep alumni event that very spring.

"David," I said, "you should know something—I know your grandfather. I grew up at Angwin, California. I know your whole family clan—your great grandparents, your great uncles and aunts, and your father's relative, Delmer, was one of my best friends in academy and college. I met your grandfather in April at a Prep alumni Sabbath. He told me all about the place that you just visited."

"You know my grandpa! How can that be?" David shouted to the whole carload this seemingly impossible fact. How nice to quickly have a special bond with a new student!

Being a low tide day, we spent our first day exploring tide pools on Rosario Beach.

The second morning we had an awesome surprise. Mr. Rice had arranged for us to spend the day touring Anacortes Bay on a friend's destroyer along with divers diving deep to find marine specimens. The Admiral and his wife had refurbished a ninety-three-foot destroyer (which had done active duty at Normandy in WWII). We were all waiting beside our vans when the Admiral's wife breezed by in her white Ford pickup truck. On seeing me standing in the parking lot, she rushed over—arms outstretched—and gave me an enthusiastic hug! Big surprise to the students, big surprise to both the admiral's wife and to me! Bonnie and I had been schoolmates in grade school in Oregon and again in academy in California. Neither of us knew that the other one was involved in this trip, and we had not seen each other in years.

Bonnie and her admiral husband were great hosts. Even though we had some rain, it was a great day. The divers brought up about thirty sea life specimens from down under, so the Cypress students had a wonderful day of real hands-on science. When the rain did come in earnest, we were invited into the galley and served hot chocolate, hot soup, and crackers.

These happy, unexpected experiences demonstrated to everyone in our group the extra-specialness of belonging to the world-wide family of Seventh-day Adventists. It is indeed a unique privilege to have an Adventist education and to belong to the Adventist world family!

29.
WHEN THEY RING THOSE GOLDEN BELLS

The saga of the "Golden Bells" actually begins with the flashing of the silver chimes! Cypress Adventist School was blessed with two great music teachers in a row. For the first, Rita Jo Sawyer, we arranged for a donor to purchase a set of Tone Chimes. They were such a hit for our music program that we decided to reach for the stars and go after a set of Hand Bells. The Mallmark Company offered a "sponsor a bell program." They figured the average cost per bell for the base three octave set of thirty-seven with each donor's name embedded in a bell handle.

We sent out info to all parents and constituents. We visited church boards, and, with God's blessing, we raised the needed $12,000 in five weeks. Later, Alex Gagiu assumed the music teacher role at Cypress Adventist School.

Hand bells became a central feature in the yearly Christian Education Day Sabbaths in area churches. On these occasions, students played major roles. Mr. Roberts, the upper-grade teacher, opened with a warm hymn-variation piano prelude, students led in praise songs, followed with choirs, the reading of scriptures, and bell ringing. One Sabbath as we set up the bell choir tables, an eighth-grader threw me a big challenge: "Last month I timed your sermon at twenty minutes! Why don't you try for eighteen minutes today?" I actually did it!

When I look back over the years and see the many places where the "Golden Bells" were invited to play, I can only exclaim with the prophet of old, "What has God wrought?" (Num. 23:23, ESV).

The "Golden Bells" performed in the following Adventist church venues to great blessing: Ballard, Edmonds, Green Lake, Shoreline, Volunteer Park, North Creek Fellowship, Lynnwood-Everett Spanish, Seattle Korean, Auburn Camp Meeting, and Washington Conference Music Festival Sabbaths at AAA.

In addition to enriching area Adventist church services, the "Golden Bells" were central to many school programs: Cypress Christmas, the education fair, and spring programs.

The "Golden Bells" also reached out to enrich both city and state, charming audiences at Bellevue City of Lights, the Lynnwood City Hall Christmas Tree Lightning, Barnes and Noble school holiday concerts, and Washington State Fair School Band Stand Concerts at Puyallup.

It's amazing the impact that dedicated Christian teachers and students can have when we work hard, pull together, and are willing to follow wherever God may lead!

NOTE: The title of this chapter is borrowed from an old hymn, but it was infused by our experience with a new meaning.

30.
CATCHING THE BEAT OF ADVENTIST EDUCATION

My alarm rang early. Must I get up? It's the weekend! Why can't I just turn my tired body over and sleep in? Then it dawned on me. Today is the fifth and final Education Sabbath in our constituent churches. The beat of Adventist Education roused me! Get up and get ready! Go over my sermon notes! Drive twenty-five miles through urban traffic and pick up two bell choir members! Unload tables, pads, and hand bells! Set up the tables and pads! Spread the tablecloths! Arrange the bells! Rehearse one last time with the voice choir! Help the music teacher get all the kids in order and in place!

At 11:00 everyone was in place. The students, dressed in black and white—a microcosm of the twelve ethnic groups making up our school family—filed up to the front to lead praise songs. You could feel the audience catch their breath at the sight of them! It would be hard to find a happier group of children anywhere on planet earth! And how they sang! The bell choir, dressed in scarlet uniforms, followed with "Be Thou My Vision" and "God's Train" (a number with great sound effects)! The speech choir introduced the theme of the day, "It Takes a Village to Mentor a Child," with the skit "Peter in Prison—Rhoda at the Door."

My sermon recapped the story in Acts 12. Someone at the New Testament church in Jerusalem noticed Rhoda. Someone invited her to the prayer meeting for Peter's deliverance! Someone gave her the position of responsibility to guard the door! Rhoda became the heroine of faith in one of the greatest miracle stories in the Bible. Next, I shared three stories of people who were significant mentors to me in my elementary, academy, and college years. I closed with a call for mentors. "The voices of the Village children are calling today: 'Where are the keepers of the Village?' Will there be an answer? That is up to you and me!"

Church was over. As I walked down the center aisle to greet the congregation, I momentarily stopped at the sound booth to return the lapel mic. I didn't make it to the door. A hand touched my shoulder. I had noticed three out-of-work teachers in the audience. The one who touched me was one of them. Words tumbled out, "I walked in today feeling low. I don't have a clue about what I'm going to do next year! It was providential that I came here today. In this last hour, I've recaptured my vision to be an Adventist teacher!"

Another hand beckoned to me from across the church. Out poured another story:

"This last winter I was diagnosed with cancer. I didn't like the way I was treated in a large hospital here. Somehow, I ended up at Loma Linda. They not only cured my cancer, but they cared about me as a person. I just got home. When I awoke this morning, I thought I would visit an Adventist church. I knew that you Adventists had great hospitals, but I had no idea that you had schools too. Your students were wonderful! I'm coming back next Sabbath."

A third hand motioned for me to come. His story went like this:

"I can't believe what I witnessed today. Your kids actually looked happy up there! About twenty-five years ago I went to an Adventist boarding school. That was in the legalistic age: just rules, rules, rules. When my buddies and I graduated, we vowed never to darken the door of an Adventist church again! I'm the first one to venture back. By the way, who's that Gillespie guy?"

(I had referred to Gillespie's Valugenesis Study and how student attitudes had changed with a new focus on "grace orientation.")

"I would like more information about these positive changes."

The church was now empty. As I went my homeward way, my whole being was reverberating with the beat of Adventist Education!

My whole heart was singing with its music—singing about the opportunities it gives to my current students *now!* singing about its ability to recharge a discouraged teacher! singing about its drawing power to a new seeker! singing about its magnetic pull on a former member! singing because, I myself, have a part in "the nicest work ever committed to mortals" (to quote Ellen White)! And, yes, singing in anticipation that you, the reader, may catch the beat of Adventist Education and hear its music!

31.
CAN I COME TO YOUR SCHOOL?

It was Friday morning just before Labor Day, our fifth day of school. My secretary said, "There's a child on the phone asking for the principal." I picked up the phone.

"Mr. Principal, I'm Jerry, can I come to your school?"

I responded, "Well, I hope so. Do you live nearby? May I speak with your mom or dad?"

Jerry continued, "We just arrived from the Marshall Islands. I'm all alone at mamma's friend's house. Can I call tomorrow?"

The next day we set up a meeting time for 10:00 Sunday. It took forty-five minutes and three bus transfers for Jerry and his parents to reach Cypress Adventist School. They had jobs in food service, but no car, and no place of their own in which to live.

Jerry's principal from the Marshall Islands was here in Washington state on vacation. He gave Jerry high marks, recommending that Jerry be placed in sixth grade, my home room. Early Tuesday morning, Jerry appeared at school, proudly showing me a book of bus tickets, eager to enter school. They had found an apartment near the bus transfer station where Jerry could board just one bus which would get him to our school.

"If you can take me home today, mamma and daddy want to talk with you."

We entered his second-floor apartment. The open bedroom doors showed no beds or dressers, only sleeping bags rolled out on the floor. The living areas had no furniture! Jerry's mom welcomed me, saying, "Nice floor" gesturing for me to sit down. She made another gesture to the picture window overlooking a green belt (a thin but dense strip of trees, separating the apartment from the neighboring subdivision), saying, "Nice view." Jerry disappeared into the kitchen, momentarily returning with a coffee cup of orange juice and a saucer with a piece of cheesecake. "Daddy's a dessert maker," he remarked.

Acting as translator, Jerry helped to unfold the story of his family's journey to the United States and their desire for Jerry to receive a quality education. Mom began, "Adventist Schools much better than Island government schools, so we want Jerry to continue in one here."

Noticing the complete lack of furniture, I quietly said to Jerry, "You've just arrived in the United States, and I didn't see any furniture. Is

> *I was stunned! All they felt they needed were some coat hangers!*

there anything we could help you with?" Jerry spoke briefly with his mother in Chinese, then started drawing in his notebook and then showed me the picture. I was stunned! All they felt they needed were some coat hangers! I chose not to ask about money. Anyone wanting an Adventist education that bad deserved to be in our school!

Two days later, Jerry handed me a legal envelope. Inside were five crisp new $100 bills. The Cypress staff quickly rallied their support: a like-new circular couch, a dining room table and chairs, a study desk and chair for Jerry, and several dozen new plastic coat hangers.

Everyone quickly fell in love with Jerry. He was warm, open, friendly, and radiantly happy for the privilege to attend another Adventist School. It wasn't easy! While Jerry spoke and understood English quite well, writing it was another story! Our first task on Jerry's first morning was to create a new sentence with each new spelling word of the week. Jerry appeared overwhelmed.

"Mr. D., I don't know the meaning of the words!"

"Jerry, I don't expect you to do everything perfectly. You've indicated that you wish to try the same work as all the others. How many definitions can you remember at a time?"

"About three."

That was our beginning. There probably never was a student who worked any harder! Jerry made rapid progress in this supportive environment. Jerry loved to sing. His strong boy soprano voice held through his eighth-grade year. We all rejoiced, including Jerry, when He took the leading vocal role in the spring musical, doing "a smashing job."

Jerry's parents spoke Chinese and understood only a little English. They were not Seventh-day Adventists, and they did not own a car. Here we could see Jerry's influence. On many a Sabbath morning, Jerry and his parents boarded a transit bus and worshipped at the nearest Adventist church located in Edmonds.

Jerry taught our school family many things: sacrifice, cooperation, dedication to make the most of every opportunity, and embracing those around you. Jerry has kept in touch. At last contact, Jerry was enrolled in college in Japan. "Jerry, may your tribe increase!"

32.

THE ADVENTIST DILEMMA

The previous portions of my memoir have dealt with God's providential leading in my growing up years in Adventism, followed by His manifold blessings throughout my career working in the Adventist system for nearly fifty years.

In this concluding chapter, I feel that I must explore a complex issue that has proved a major stumbling block for many. Often, we tend to get caught up with the volume of online criticisms of what's wrong with the church, the system! Yes, I admit, we do face many challenges! The system is not perfect! Nor are the personnel running it!

Early in my college years, a church history teacher had us memorize the following quotation, "Enfeebled and defective as it may appear, the church is the only object upon which God bestows in a special sense His supreme regard" (Ellen White, *Acts of the Apostles*, p. 12).

One of my early assignments was pastoring a small church in Nebraska. The folks wanted to have a homecoming Sabbath, inviting past members back to celebrate God's leading over the years. Just before services began, a stern-faced gentleman appeared. While he walked around, a veteran member warned me, "Watch out for that brother! He caused us a lot of trouble in our early days!" He soon made his way to where I was welcoming guests and, with a sober face and stern voice, challenged me. "I see that you are not reading the Spirit of Prophecy. You're not preaching the straight testimony here. As I walked around, I noticed several wedding rings and several ladies wearing lipstick! Do some still bring meat to potluck dinner?"

> "We did not come today to nitpick and criticize one another. If that's why you came, then you're not welcome!"

I replied, "Brother, we invited guests here today to remember and rejoice in God's leading in our past. We did not come today to nitpick and criticize one another. As I read Ellen White, she says that our greatest sin is the spirit of criticism. If that's why you came, then you're not welcome!"

He hastily grabbed his coat and Bible and left. I was then told that he was an "off-shoot." The old-timers were very relieved that he was gone.

In the New Testament Church, which Jesus Christ Himself founded, perfect harmony did not exist. The disciples quarreled among themselves. All the disciples forsook Jesus on the crucifixion weekend! Peter and Paul had a heated public disagreement. Paul and Barnabas separated over a personnel decision. And yet the Day of Pentecost had brought a genuine conversion experience to each disciple. Each disciple became empowered with the gifts of the Holy Spirit.

In spite of the fact that the early church appeared enfeebled and defective, under the unifying power of God's Spirit, the church went forward, having a united sense of mission, taking the gospel to the whole world in the first century!

As the epistle to the Colossians closes, Paul, who is in chains for the gospel, a prisoner in Rome, mentions that Mark, cousin of Barnabas, is with him. That's a precious verse, evidence of a true reconciliation! Unity of purpose in proclaiming the love of Jesus to our world does indeed change hearts and bring oneness of purpose.

In contrast to my opening story in this chapter, I share the following powerful experience. For nearly twenty years I was blessed to be a member of the Oregon Adventist Men's Chorus. We sang three times at the 2010 GC session. After our final concert, an African delegate approached an OAMC leader saying, "While you were singing, God impressed me to invite you to South Africa!" That's how the International Brotherhood Tour was born!

Several African brothers opened their hearts to us. We were aware of the apartheid history and its horrible effects. As a group, we determined that we would model total "oneness in Christ"—we would share the same guestrooms, ride the same busses, stand shoulder to shoulder on the concert stages, and be totally ONE with our black male chorus brothers!

Behold what followed! At our first lunch, I sat beside the senior member of the Botswana Black Male Chorus. With tears in his eyes and voice he said, "You will never know how much the coming of you Americans means to us Africans. In all of my seventy-seven years, this is my first experience of having equality with a white man!"

Instantly, I knew why I came to Africa!

One day at practice, we Americans were having trouble getting the African rhythms. My seatmate was a powerfully built African brother. He spoke out, "Stand up! Link elbows! We Africans sing with our whole bodies!"

We stood up! We linked elbows! We sang, and we got it! Praise the Lord!

Imagine the impact that we made—black and white standing shoulder to shoulder on the concert stages of the major cities of South Africa! When an African conductor stepped to the podium and we sang several songs in African languages, the crowds went wild!

On the final leg of our bus trip, Brother D, who sat across the aisle from me, said, "You'll never know how much this trip means to us Africans! For years we Africans have longed to participate with our Caucasian brothers and sisters! You Americans coming has fulfilled our dream and helped us proclaim to our whole country that Adventists are NOT RACISTS!" Brother D died last summer. I'm eternally grateful that we helped make his dream come true!

As you listened to the two stories that I've shared with you in this concluding chapter, I pray that you will have discovered the positive solution to the trauma involved in meeting and surmounting the Adventist Dilemma! Then you also may be ready to discover the JOY awaiting you in participating in the Adventist Journey, finding it to be a foretaste of heaven!

33. EPILOGUE

A MILLENNIUM OF AFFIRMATION

It's the first evening in heaven! The vast throng which no one can number finishes the banquet meal of the Marriage Supper of the Lamb. As Gabriel leads the angel choir in after-dinner music, the crowd becomes aware that the head table is empty. The curtain slowly rises. A throbbing expectancy beats in every breast! Out steps the Son of God, Adam, and Eve. They take three chairs as a giant video screen descends. Lights dim.

There God appears, shaping Adam from the dust! And then He puts His lips on Adam's lips. The audience gasps as "Mr. Universe" awakens! Animals stream by two by two as Adam names them. Adam wonders, *Is there no counterpart for me?*

Adam drifts into a deep sleep. God takes out His scalpel, opens Adam's side, and gently removes a rib to form the woman—Eve is her name. "Ms. World" awaits, a hint of a smile on her face, as "Mr. Universe" awakes. Adam cries out, "Is she really for me?" The heavenly throng bursts into applause!

Applause fades into apprehension as Eve gazes at the tree! The winged serpent hands Eve the fruit! Will she take it? Fear chills every spine as Eve slowly reaches out her hand, grasping the forbidden object!

We watch as the guilty pair leaves Eden. Tears well up in every eye! Men break into cold sweat as thorns and thistles grow! Women weep with Eve as she cries out in childbirth! Then every man exudes Adam's pride as he holds Earth's first child!

All heaven then walks the dusty trails of Earth with Adam and Eve. We sense their sadness as flowers fade. We cringe as the first sacrificial lamb is offered! We grieve with them in their trauma as they learn that Abel has died! We weep with them as the rebel Cain, who has murdered his brother, callously turns and walks his separate way!

We share their pain as we walk the way of sin that both they and we have chosen. In spite of the way that sin warps our world, we find hope with them through the promise of the Redeemer to come!

Somehow, as the hologram of Earth's first family plays out, all critical, condemning thoughts toward Eve and Adam cease, for we have walked Earth's way with them.

Heaven has now become a safe place for Adam, for Eve, for each of us!

I've never thought that God needed a thousand years to judge the wicked or to convince the saints of His justice. I've come to the realization that the main reason for the thousand years is to have a millennium of affirmation so that heaven will be a safe place for every saint! Heaven is big enough, there are sufficient angels to arrange the space, and there is time enough for every saved individual to have his or her "THIS IS YOUR LIFE" moment.

"Then I shall know fully, even as I am fully known" (1 Cor. 13:12, NIV). Then the spirit of acceptance and affirmation will dominate all heaven! Grief recovery will be complete! God will wipe away all tears! Heaven will now be safe for everyone!

REPRISE

As you have walked along many pathways of Adventist Education with me in my memoir, as you have experienced the countless ways that Christian education has blessed both me and my family, as you have watched the amazing enrichment of numerous students in the mentoring process, it is my hope and prayer that you, the readers, will have reclaimed and recaptured the value of this priceless gift that God has bestowed upon His remnant people. Adventist Education has double aims: it is earthly and heavenly. Remember with me some quotations from the pen of Ellen White: "True education means more than the pursual of a certain course of study.... It prepares the student for the joy of service in this world and for the higher joy of wider service in the world to come" (*Education*, p. 13).

"To restore in man the image of his Maker, to bring him back to the perfection in which he was created, to promote the development of body, mind, and soul, that the divine purpose in his creation might be realized—this was to be the work of redemption. This is the object of education, the great object of life" (*Education*, pp. 15, 16).

The trials of our faith-walk on Earth will be worth it all!

"It will (indeed) be worth it all, when we see Jesus!"

BIBLIOGRAPHY

Gillespie, V. Bailey and Niels-Erik A. Andreasen. *Project Affirmation: Perspectives on Values*. Riverside, CA : La Sierra University Press, 1993.

Stuart, Jesse. *The Thread that Runs So True*. New York, NY: Scribner, 1958.

White, Ellen G. *Acts of the Apostles*. Mountain View, CA: Pacific Press Publishing Association, 1911

———. *Christ's Object Lessons*. Washington, D.C.: Review and Herald Publishing Association, 1941.

———. *Education*. Mountain View, CA: Pacific Press Publishing Association, 1952.

We invite you to view the complete
selection of titles we publish at:
www.TEACHServices.com

We encourage you to write us
with your thoughts about this,
or any other book we publish at:
info@TEACHServices.com

TEACH Services' titles may be purchased in
bulk quantities for educational, fund-raising,
business, or promotional use.
bulksales@TEACHServices.com

Finally, if you are interested in seeing
your own book in print, please contact us at:
publishing@TEACHServices.com
We are happy to review your manuscript at no charge.

www.ingramcontent.com/pod-product-compliance
Lightning Source LLC
Chambersburg PA
CBHW070541170426
43200CB00011B/2506

PRAISE FOR
Faith Trek Into the Unknown

This is a book of love. Written by a man who believes in Adventist education and has the stories of miracles and divine intervention to back it up. It is a book of love because Lowell has experienced the ups and downs of being on the frontlines of the Adventist institution, he is aware of the shortcomings, and yet he uplifts the good, and continues to promote the best that Adventist education can be. The stories told here are a treasure for all who share Lowell's conviction that Adventist education is still something worth investing in.

— Pastor Kevin McGill Green Lake Adventist Church

Being a retired SDA teacher makes it easy for me to relate to the joys and challenges of Lowell's experiences working for the church. The stories in this book reveal what can happen when a person serves God and follows His leading for a lifetime. When a person stays true to God's call, refusing to get sidetracked if things get tough, he can make a difference in this world and for God. Miracles can and do happen.

— Helen Sage, Retired Teacher

Faith Trek Into the Unknown by Lowell Dunston is an intimate portrayal of the intense devotion and spiritual and social motivations of a lifelong Adventist teacher and preacher, with emphasis on the educator role. It paints a vivid picture of the tight-knit world of Adventist Church employees. Dunston's story epitomizes the culture that built the Adventist education system in North America and provides insight into that culture.

— John McLarty, Retired Pastor

Lowell Dunston has captured the immediacy and anxiety—as well as the joys—of education in the Seventh-Day Adventist Church. He personally attended one-room schools as well as moved frequently with his family so they could educate their children on larger campuses. He knew firsthand the financial sacrifices and enormous faith benefits of getting a Christian education, and also outlines in very clear prose how much dedication he and other educators demonstrated through decades of service. The personal commitment and sacrifices involved in serving as both a pastor and an educator are vividly set forth with the theme, "All His biddings are enablings."

— Karla K. Walters, Ph.D.,
Retired English Professor and High School Teacher

In *Faith Trek Into the Unknown,* Lowell Dunston provides a brief memoir of his experiences from early childhood to his present retired status somewhat plagued by annoying health issues. Always with an honest and authentic voice, he narrates how God led him and others through both joyful and stressful situations as he served as a pastor, teacher and school principal. In a clear and lively style, he emphasizes how his Christian Seventh-day Adventist upbringing, including hard work, as well as Bible study, singing songs of praise, and prayer often resulted in everyday miracles and life-changing events for not only him but also for his family, colleagues, parishioners, and students! With its emphasis on faith and joy amid the challenges of daily work life, this book is well worth reading because it encourages attention and commitment to God on every page!

— Dr. Delmer Davis,
Professor of English, Emeritus, Andrews University